The Most Important Page in the Book
(Formerly known as the Preface)

Why is this the MOST IMPORTANT PAGE IN THE BOOK? Well, the simple answer to that question is that this is where we explain how the book is laid out. Certainly, once you look at the Table of Contents you probably would get a general idea, but we really want you to understand the purpose of the book.

So, here it is...our goal is to help you be successful in your AP Human Geography class. And we really want this book to be user friendly and very flexible.

We have three simple, major goals in this book and therefore, we organized the book into three parts.

1. **Understanding AP Human Geography:** Our goal is to introduce you to the course. We explain what AP Human Geography is and how the class is organized.

2. **Understanding Your Textbook:** Our goal is to give you some reading strategies immediately, and then provide a chapter-by-chapter study tool in order to help you better comprehend what you have read.

3. **Understanding the AP Exam:** The final section is designed to help you get prepared for the AP exam. We will give you study tools and a practice exam in order to better prepare you for the test.

In essence, this study guide is like three books in one or if you like:

This book is like an amazing ice cream sandwich, with Part 2 being the incredible ice cream filling between two delicious chocolate cookies. (Please try to refrain from biting the book—it is just a yummy metaphor.)

And, let's just say for a second, you don't like chocolate and you only want ice cream! Well, you can just jump right into Part 2 of the book and sink your teeth into the middle. (Don't read too quickly or you might get an ice cream headache.)

Or if you just want one cookie, you can jump to Part 3 and prepare for the AP exam.

We believe that the beauty of the book is that it can stay with you throughout the entire year or be used whenever you want. The only thing better would be if it came in a scratch and sniff version.

Teacher's note: Both of the authors are AP Human Geography teachers with over 20 years of combined experience teaching the class. Through their years of teaching, they have included many ideas on how to structure the class. And they have tried to capture the high school mindset and to structure the book in a way that a teenager would appreciate, injecting humor at times and giving clues to important aspects of the class in simple ways.

TABLE OF CONTENTS

Advanced Placement
Study Guide

Greg Sherwin

Paul T. Gray, Jr.

Human Geography

People, Place, and Culture

Tenth Edition

Erin H. Fouberg
Northern State University

Alexander B. Murphy
University of Oregon

H. J. de Blij
Michigan State University

WILEY

To our wives

Heather Sherwin and Beth Gray

For their love and support

For our children

Carter Sherwin, Dylan Sherwin, Zach Gray, Ariston Gray,
Jenny Gray, and Grayden Winget

Go out and explore the world of opportunities

Special Thanks to

Parisa Watson

For creating the chapter review guides

Front-cover photo: © Alexander B. Murphy

Copyright © 2012 by John Wiley & Sons, Inc.

Founded in 1807, John Wiley & Sons, Inc., has been a valued source of knowledge and understanding for more than 200 years, helping people around the world meet their needs and fulfill their aspirations. Our company is built on a foundation of principles that include responsibility to the communities we serve and where we live and work. In 2008, we launched a Corporate Citizenship Initiative, a global effort to address the environmental, social, economic, and ethical challenges we face in our business. Among the issues we are addressing are carbon impact, paper specifications and procurement, ethical conduct within our business and among our vendors, and community and charitable support. For more information, please visit our website: *www.wiley.com/go/citizenship*.

ISBN 978-1-118-16686-4

Printed in the United States of America

10 9 8 7 6 5 4 3 2 1

Printed and bound by Bind-Rite/Robbinsville

PART 1: UNDERSTANDING AP HUMAN GEOGRAPHY

SECTION 1
WHAT IS HUMAN GEOGRAPHY?:
THIS AIN'T YOUR DADDY'S OR MOMMA'S GEOGRAPHY

The purpose of this section is to teach you what this class is—pretty simple and extremely important. We believe that the first step is to explain what the class isn't and then slowly give you definitions. So there are three parts to this section:

A.   This Ain't Your Daddy's or Momma's Geography!
B.   What Is Geography?
C.   What Is Human Geography?

A. This Ain't Your Daddy's or Momma's Geography!

Too many students assume they know what AP Human Geography is, but they really don't. Even more students take the class without really knowing what they've signed up for and wish they did know.

Sometimes students talk with their parents, and their parents tell them what they think the class is. Most parents think this class is something they took when they were in high school. Unfortunately, parents forget that their high school days were long ago in a world where there were no cell phones and Abraham Lincoln was still president (or for those of you with young parents perhaps Teddy Roosevelt).

We are here to tell you, *"This ain't your Daddy's or Momma's geography!"*

Despite what you might have thought, the following is a list of what this class is not.

This is not a geography coloring book class!

A lot of students assume that there will be a geography coloring book that they have to fill in countries or places with different colors. Yes, we will study maps! And yes, we will learn why different colors are used on maps. But if you thought you could get a credit in art by taking this class, you probably need to draw yourself a sad face right now.

This is not geography on Jeopardy!

You WON'T be memorizing capitals of countries and you won't be quizzed on memorization. That's geography for *Jeopardy* and that's your daddy's (or granddaddy's) geography! Many elementary and high school geography courses focus on memorizing places. And while knowing where countries are and what their capitals are is great, this class goes far beyond mere memorization of places and creates a deep-rooted understanding of the world.

This is not physical geography!

A physical geographer studies the Earth's natural phenomena such as climate, soil, plants, animals, and topography and looks for patterns and makes conclusions. Courses like Environmental Studies study these concepts.

A human geographer, while not ignoring the fact that deserts, rainfall, and the like affect the world, focuses on how peoples of the world structure their population, their cultures, and other activities. We don't study "what makes it rain"; rather, we study how PEOPLE deal with too much or too little rainfall as it relates to aspects of their lives ranging from their economic activities to their religious customs.

This is not a history class!

While geographers use history, and historians use geography, they differ fundamentally in their main approach to understanding events.

Historians use time as the framework of their courses. They study everything chronologically, starting at a certain time and moving forward. Essentially, historians ask "when" did something occur and then explain "why." Time lines are an essential component of a historical understanding.

Geographers, in contrast to historians, use space as the framework of their courses. They study everything "spatially"; that is, they use space as the foundation. Essentially, geographers are interested in "where" something is and "why" it is occurring in that particular location. (See the "Where and Why" section on page 11 for more information.)

Some further thoughts:

---

1. Being good at memorizing capitals and countries won't hurt you.
The more you know about where places are in the world, the quicker you can make connections and the better you will understand concepts. It is easier to succeed with a strong mental map.

Would you like an analogy?

Knowing where countries and other places are on a map is like bringing a large plate to class. When the teacher serves up the food (information) in class, you'll get every last bit of it on your plate. And you'll know how to separate your broccoli from your potatoes. Mmmm...knowledge. Tasty!

---

2.   Being good at science won't hurt you.

Having a rock-solid foundation (get it?) in science (physical geography) provides a good background and connections for understanding the effects of humans on the planet. But again, our focus will be on humans and their impact on the environment, and not necessarily on the science behind the impact. In other words, we will not focus on what caused the hurricane or the earthquake, but on why so many people live in hazard zones.

3.   Being good at history won't hurt you.

But just because you were good at history does not guarantee that you will do well in AP Human Geography. Many students struggle early in geography and say things like "but I usually do so well in history class."

Remember, the two courses are related, but they are different in their approaches. For history class, you need a chronological mind and you've developed that special skill over many years of history classes.

THINKING SPATIALLY!

Developing a spatial mind takes time for many students. We imagine that many of you are used to thinking historically and that you have a good chronological mind. However, this might be your first geography class, and so it might take time to get used to seeing information spatially.

But you need to think **spatially** in order to succeed. And we want you to be successful.

How about a quick lesson to begin your development of your spatial mind? All of you have no doubt seen the FedEx® logo? Here it is again.

Source: Paul T. Gray, Jr.

But have you ever noticed the arrow between the E and the x? If you haven't, look at the logo again.[1]

Now, try looking at the logo without seeing the arrow. You can't do it! This is what learning how to think spatially will do. You will see things that have been right in front of your eyes all along in a new way. This is the magic of thinking like a geographer.

THINKING SPATIALLY (PART 2)

Now how about this sign? It's just an interesting sign, right?

Source: Paul T. Gray, Jr.

No, the sign is almost audibly shouting geographical components. Why does the sign exist? Why is there no liquor? Where is there a place that would have no liquor?

Once you learn how to think geographically, you'll see signs like this and you'll be forced to think about them! (See page 266 in your textbook on how to interpret this sign spatially. Do you have a hypothesis?)

FINAL THOUGHTS:

As we stated before, this could be your first geography class. Be patient. There will be terms that you will learn for the first time. Don't panic. Learning to think spatially might also take some time. Don't worry. Realize that this is a new experience and that with time you'll get it. Many students struggle in the beginning, but once they get it, they will never lose it—just like the FedEx logo.

---

[1] From the work of John Stilgoe. Visit the link below to see more on how to interpret landscapes using Harvard professor John Stilgoe's work. CBS *60 Minutes* episode called "The Eyes Have It," January 5, 2004. http://www.cbsnews.com/stories/2003/12/31/60minutes/main590907.shtml?tag=mncol;lst;1

B. What Is Geography?

By now, we hope that you have begun to shape an idea of what AP Human Geography isn't (and have gotten a little bit of an idea of what it is). But let's take a step back. Perhaps the best way to begin to understand "What is AP Human Geography?" is to begin with "What is Geography?"

And the best approach to that is to start with a few definitions.

Geography:

- is the scientific study of the Earth's surface.
- studies the interactions between people and their physical environments.
- focuses on the locational and spatial variations of phenomena, both human and nonhuman (so-called natural or physical/biological).
- is descriptive, that is, describes a phenomenon (an occurrence), where it is located, and how it is related to other phenomena (occurrences).
- identifies regions (again, both human/cultural and physical/biological regions).
- describes, analyzes, explains, and interprets.

Charles Fuller, former geography professor at Triton College, has used the following description of geography in his course syllabi:

Geography is the systematic study of the spatial patterns of all phenomena on or near the Earth's surface. Its primary methodology is spatial analysis, which asks two basic questions: **where** are things located (spatial), and why are they located where they are (analysis—**why there**). Its primary tool of communication is the map.

Stop for a second. Read the definition again. Notice the use of **the words where** and **why there** in the definition. Remember, "Where" and "Why There" are the essential questions in the course! (Again, make sure you go to the "Where and Why" section on page 11.)

Now, let's see how the idea of spatial analysis is described using those two questions. "Where" gives us the spatial part, and "Why There" gives us the analysis.

One other word worth taking note of is "pattern." Geographers scan maps to look for patterns or instances of phenomena (occurrences). Where is this occurring? Where isn't it occurring? Is there a pattern? Why does this pattern exist?

To get a better understanding of how geography works, please read the following essay about Chicago and geography.

Defining Geography: What Is It? What Does It Mean?

By James Marran

Many people perceive geography as simply an exercise in place location. That means being able to answer a single question about a place: Where is it? If, for example, Chicago is identified as a city in northeastern Illinois on the southwestern shore of Lake Michigan, that information has indeed answered the "Where is it?" question. To be even more accurate, data on the city's latitudinal and longitudinal coordinates could be given showing it at 41°49'N, 87°37'W.

Even though such identifiers about Chicago's location are accurate, they bring the inquirer only to the threshold of really getting the total "geographic" picture because there are other more important and more interesting questions to pose and answer about places. Chicago becomes far more meaningful when it is understood in the context of the answers to these questions:

- Why is it where it is?
- How did it get there?
- What does it look like?
- Where is it in relation to other places?
- Why did it grow so large?
- How is it connected to other places in its region, its country, its continent, and the world?
- How does it interact with other places?

Learning the answers to these questions begins to give Chicago dimension and meaning since they identify both its physical (natural) and human (cultural) features. They also provide a context for studying the spatial characteristics of the city by making clear both its site (its physical setting) and its situation (its location in relation to other places). More importantly, the interaction between Chicago's physical and cultural features helps explain its role as an immensely diverse urban magnet that for almost two centuries has drawn people from across the world to live and work in its neighborhoods and the hinterland (i.e., suburbs) beyond. Photographs and maps showing the tracks that lace the city's rail yards like so many scrimshaw etchings and mile-long runways accommodating thousands of flights daily at O'Hare International Airport reveal a tapestry of transportation networks moving people, goods, ideas, and services to and from all corners of the Earth. And the communications aerials atop the Sears (Willis) Tower and the Hancock Building in the central business district (downtown) send images and words that inform, entertain, and challenge people around the globe. As a manufacturing core and marketplace, Chicago provides a commercial function that helps make the economy of the United States the world's largest and strongest.

Certainly a list inventorying the city's role that derives from its location could go on and on, but the point is clear. Wherever a place is only marks the beginning of giving it definition and establishing its importance among other places. By examining the spatial aspects of a place's location and how the people living there function and make their living confirm that geography is not so much about the memorization of facts but also asking questions, solving problems and making informed decisions about the physical and human complexities of the planet.

So, why is Chicago a large city in the United States? It is safe to say that it is due to its geography. But remember that its geography encompasses both its physical setting (an inland port city) and its human features: cultural, political and economic. As a result of those combined geographic forces, Chicago became a transportation hub (center), a center for manufacturing, and a dominant city in the United States. And truly, this essay helps us bridge the gap between "What is Geography?" and "What is Human Geography?"

C. What Is Human Geography?

Human Geography is one of the major divisions of geography; the spatial analysis of human population, its cultures, activities, and landscapes.

-Fouberg, Murphy, and de Blij

This is not a bad definition, so let's break down it down:

- We know what geography is, so we're off to a good start!
- We have looked at the terms *spatial* and *analysis* already.
- The rest of the definition is pretty simple to understand.

But let's expand on the definition so that we can get a really good understanding about what you will be studying in class.

Using the spatial perspective, Human Geographers look at **where** something occurs, search for patterns, and span most of the social studies disciplines to answer the **why there** question.

Therefore, in the end, students in Human Geography will study history, religion, politics, economics, sociology and other social studies subjects. Geography (through maps, charts, etc.) shows us where something occurs. Then we work with the other social studies subjects when they help us answer the **why there** question.

Human Geography covers all of the social studies subjects under the sun. If only there was a visual to illustrate the importance of Human Geography. And you've probably guessed it—there is such a graphic:

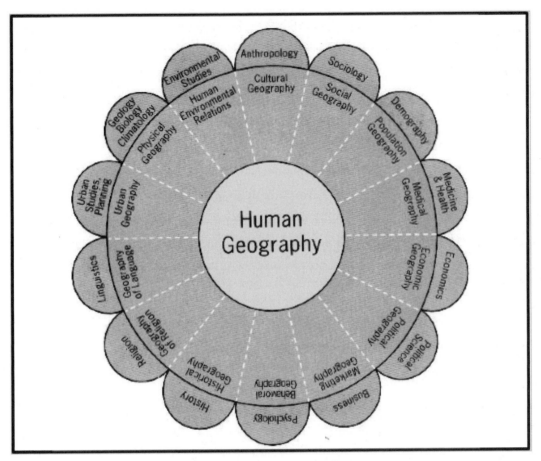

Source: de Blij and Murphy, *Human Geography, Seventh Edition,* John Wiley & Sons, Inc.

In the end, Human Geography provides the foundation for understanding fundamental similarities and differences between people culturally, politically, economically, and socially through a spatial perspective. It is a capstone course that will help you in other classes in your academic career. In fact, we like to think that just like the globe it will make you well-rounded.

Let's recap. You should now know what Human Geography is not; you should have a sense of what geography is; and finally you should understand what, specifically, Human Geography is. But just in case you need some more detail, we've included a small sampling of topics covered in Human Geography:

- Students will study the conflict between Spanish speakers in California and English speakers on one scale, but they will also learn about other conflicts such as the one between Flemish and French speakers in Belgium.

- Students will learn about where their food comes from and how it is produced. Did you know your strawberry shake from a fast-food restaurant does not have one strawberry in it? It does, however, have over 45 chemicals that make it taste like strawberries.[2]

- Students will study transportation network patterns and the impact the Federal Highway Act of 1956 had on the development of the United States, comparing it with the lack of development of a transcontinental railroad in Africa and its impact on the economy.

- Students will study the conflict between secularism and religion in the world today, how Islam got to Indonesia, how Confucianism blended with Buddhism in China, and how Catholicism and Protestantism didn't blend in Northern Ireland.

- Students will study how demographic shifts will change American politics in the next couple of decades. For example, Hispanics will become the majority in the United States by 2040 or so. Whites will be the largest minority followed by African Americans. How will this change electoral politics? To what states will federal monies flow during and after these demographic shifts? What policies will be changed?

---

[2] Eric Schlosser, *Fast Food Nation: The Dark Side of the American Meal* (New York: HarperCollins Books, 2002), pp. 125–126.

WHERE AND WHY THERE:
THE ESSENTIAL QUESTIONS OF AP HUMAN GEOGRAPHY

As the saying goes, "You are nowhere without geography!" The best advice for you throughout the entire year is to learn to always ask "where" and "why there." So whether you have read a section of notes, looked at a map, or studied a chart, stop yourself and ask yourself the "where" and "why there" questions.

Here are the basic steps:

- Think about **where** the pattern exists.
- Look for **where** the pattern doesn't exist.
- Then start asking yourself **why there**.

Both questions involve challenging skills, but admittedly figuring out the "why there" can be a great adventure requiring students (and teachers) to ponder all the different possibilities on why a pattern exists. Sometimes the answer is simple, and as the year goes on and you learn more about the world, you will start to make more connections faster—much as happens when you upgrade your Internet speed!

SECTION 2
WHY EVERYONE NEEDS TO TAKE HUMAN GEOGRAPHY:
IT'S A SMALLER WORLD AFTER ALL

The purpose of this section is to get you excited about taking the most important class in your life! Truly, there are only a few classes that you will take in your lifetime that will give you information that will stay with you the rest of your years. Human Geography is one of those courses.

We've divided this section into five parts:

A.   Introduction: You Need This Class!
B.   The Way It Used to Be and Why Americans Are Geographically Challenged
C.   Americans and Geography Today
D.   Conclusion: You Need This Class!
E.   Whatever You Do, Don't Take Our Word for It: Read What Students Have to Say

---

A. Introduction: You Need This Class!

We live in an era of globalization and interdependence, with countries and people interacting with each other at a more regular and rapid rate. As the Disney song goes, "It's a small world after all," and with technology becoming an integral part of everyday life, the world continues to shrink. So, in fact it is a smaller and smaller world after all (there is actually a concept we will learn later called *time–space compression* that geographers use to illustrate this idea). Dr. Michael P. Peterson at the Department of Geography/Geology, University of Nebraska at Omaha, summarizes the idea of globalization and the importance of geography in today's world:

> In a world so shrunken in distance and time that you can almost instantly communicate with any other city on any other continent, and in which you can fly to virtually its remotest corner in a matter of hours, a knowledge of differing peoples and places can no longer be considered the luxury of a few, but is, instead, a necessity of every individual. Our interdependence is so complete that business decisions taken in Tokyo and Singapore have repercussions in Copenhagen and Peoria. Just to stay abreast of world events, requires that we learn not only where these events are occurring, but also why they are taking place and how they will impact on our lives. Such considerations are the very essence of geography.

Let's see if we can get you to try to digest this quote by thinking about it bit by bit.

First, ask yourself these questions:

1.   **What more important course is there for you to take in a post-September 11 world?**
2.   **What is going to get you better prepared to compete in a global marketplace?**

3. **What is going to better prepare you to deal with the diversity of the workplace in America today?**

Now reread the quote again—stop and chew on each part. After you think about these questions and pose your own, you should come to the conclusion that geography most effectively teaches these concepts. It is a smaller world after all, and geography is one of the few courses specifically designed to prepare you for this world. Thinking geographically is important individually; however thinking and acting geographically could also be a matter of national security and economic survival at a grander scale!

B. The Way It Used to Be and Why Americans Are Geographically Challenged

Americans are geographically challenged. We don't know much about geography, and geography was never a pressing issue in American education. Why is that? Well, the irony is that the actual geography of North America has allowed the people who live there to not learn geography—in other words, to be geographically ignorant.

The United States (and Canada) has historically been isolated by political borders and physical geography. Think about the twentieth century for a second. Due to the luxury of its location in the Western Hemisphere, the United States was late in getting involved in two world wars. Why?

Because we were separated from the conflict—our geography isolated us. Separated by two oceans and with no country in turmoil on our borders, we could afford to watch troubles unfold and think about whether or not to get involved and when.

And yes, Pearl Harbor did bring the United States into World War II, but think about that attack for a moment. Hawaii, at the time, was a territory. Nestled in the Pacific Ocean, Hawaii was the best geographic target for Japan to attack, but Hawaii was far removed from the continental United States. Think again for a second. While the Japanese were able to attack Pearl Harbor, where else in the United States did they attack? And why didn't Japan take control of Hawaii after the attack? Again the answer lies in American geography.

According to Russell Bova, in a book titled, *How the World Works*:

> no war has been fought on American soil since the Civil War, and the last time foreign troops fought on American territory was the War of 1812. Americans have experienced terrorist attacks on the homeland, such as the September 11, 2001 attacks on the World Trade Center and the Pentagon, but no American alive today has ever had foreign soldiers march across his or her property, has ever had to hide in a shelter while bombs rained from above, or has ever experienced the death of a child on U.S. soil at the hands of an enemy army.[3]

---

[3] *How the World Works: A Brief Study of International Relations* (Longman, 2009), pp. 101–102. New York.

Side Note: The Japanese tried using unmanned hydrogen balloon bombs to attack the United States during World War II. The goal was for these balloons to explode in North America and create forest fires. Over 9000 balloon bombs were launched, and they took three to four days to get to the United States. Only about 1000 made it to North America. (See Karen Vigil, "Floating Death: WWII Terrorism Against U.S. Mainland Nearly Remains A Secret," *Pueblo Chieftain* (March 12, 2002).

So yes, we are telling you that Americans could afford to be geographically ignorant because our geography has protected us!

However, it is a smaller world after all, and the attacks on September 11 have proven that in a shrinking world with more interconnections, geographic isolation is no longer an option. Dr. Peterson's quote on page 12 illustrates the need for geography today.

As geographer Charles Fuller once stated:

The World has become a more crowded, more interconnected, more volatile, and more unstable place. If education cannot help students see beyond themselves and better understand the interdependent nature of our world, then each new generation will remain ignorant, and its capacity to live competently and responsibly will be dangerously diminished.

It has been over a decade since September 11 and you would think Americans, especially young Americans 18 to 24 years of age, would know more about the world today. Well, think again…

C. Americans and Geography Today

There was a phrase to describe American's geographic ignorance in the past. It went, "War is God's way of teaching Americans geography."[4] And whether it was Germany or Japan, Korea or Vietnam, we Americans, in the past, seemingly DID become interested in foreign countries and geography when we became involved in a conflict. We wanted to learn about where our soldiers were and who we were fighting. Yet, that was your parents' and your grandparents' generations. Today, we have gone from bad to worse! Today, we don't even learn about the countries that we're at war with!!

According to a National Geographic study conducted in 2006[5]:

- ***Only 37% of young Americans could find Iraq on a map***—though U.S. troops have been there since 2003.

---

[4] This quote is often attributed to Ambrose Bierce on the Internet, but according to the Ambrose Bierce website (donswaim.com), there is no record of him writing this quote.

[5] http://www.nationalgeographic.com/roper2006/findings.html

- *Almost 9 out of 10 young Americans (88%) could NOT find Afghanistan on a map of Asia*—this despite the presence of U.S. troops in the country since October 2001 and despite the fact that it is the longest conflict in American history.[6]

- *Three-quarters (75%) of young Americans CANNOT find Iran on a map*—this despite Iran being included in the "Axis of Evil" in 2002 by George W. Bush (the other two countries were Iraq and North Korea).

- *Yep, you guessed it. Seven out of ten young Americans could NOT find North Korea on a map*—what good is it having an Axis of Evil if you don't know where the evil is?

"War. What is it good for?" So goes the lyrics to Edwin Starr's 1969 protest song. "Absolutely nothing" goes the response, and given that Americans can't find countries we are fighting in or have concerns about it seems fairly accurate. Oh yeah, and China, you know that really large country with the largest population on the planet—how did young Americans fare with China?

- *Seven in ten (69%) young Americans can find China on a map!*

YES! It seems that China is one of the countries outside of North America that we can find. But hold on a minute: young Americans still have a lot to learn about China, which is one of the most economically and politically dominant countries in the world. According to the survey, few (18%) Americans know that Mandarin Chinese is the most widely spoken native language in the world; 74% say it is English.

Do these results perhaps reflect a little ethnocentrism? **Ethnocentrism** is a strong belief that your culture is the center of the universe. It was noted in the survey that Americans greatly overestimated the United States' population, thinking it was close to China's. Why? Because we're America and we're number 1—that's ethnocentrism. China's population is actually four times larger than the United States!

There was a time when U.S. students could be completely ethnocentric and isolated. Remember that our borders isolated us and the United States had hegemony (that is, political, economic, and cultural dominance of the world). For decades, the United States would act and other countries would have to react. Basically, these relationships came down to the United States saying "jump" and other countries asking "how high?" We like to call it the "John Wayne School of Foreign Policy"; ask your parents or grandparents about John Wayne and you'll get the idea.

However, we believe that in the twenty-first century, the world has changed. The United States is a strong world power with huge dominance in the world, but its hegemony is in question as other countries are rising (China in particular). It is just one more reason why we feel that AP Human Geography is the best suited class for students today. Do you need some more reasons? Keep on reading!

---

[6] This is if you use the Gulf of Tonkin incident as the starting point for the Vietnam War (August 6, 1964.) U.S. military involvement ended on 15 August 1973.

Side Note: Are you smarter than the average 18-24-year-old American? Go take the Geography test yourself (see: http://www.nationalgeographic.com/roper2006).

D. Conclusion: You Need This Class!

Students in AP Human Geography learn about the world. Remember the questions we posed to you at the beginning of this section:

1. **What more important course is there for you to take in a post-September 11 world?**
2. **What is going to get you better prepared to compete in a global marketplace?**
3. **What is going to better prepare you to deal with the diversity of the workplace in America today?**

Okay, let's add two more:

1. **Have you ever read a news story on the Internet or heard one on TV?**
2. **Have you ever wondered why they are doing that over there?**

You are not alone, but after this class you will have a much better grip on the world around you. The best comments we get from students is that they finally understand the news. Instead of the news being a series of unrelated events in unknown places, now students have background and understanding.

But don't take our word for it; read what students who have taken the course have to say.

E. Whatever You Do, Don't Take Our Word for It: Read What Students Have to Say

We believe that this is the greatest class ever created. But we understand if you are a bit skeptical about this claim. So, don't take our words for it; here are some quotes from students who took the class.

"AP Human Geography was one of the first classes to open my eyes to the global community and help me begin to understand how interconnected the world is. This course helped me pick my university major, Political Science, and is part of the reason why I am in South Korea teaching English today."   —Olivia Darmali, student 2003

"Taking this course was important because it taught me how to think on a larger scale, not just about my community or my home, but about the world as a whole. It opened my eyes to ethnicities and different cultures and to how they function with respect to the world."

—Prem Vaikuntapathi, 2010

"On my first day of AP Human Geography, I was told that this class would make everything on the news make more sense. I didn't see how that could be possible, but sure enough it was. AP Human

Geography was the most relevant class I took in high school. I still reference the class all these years later."   —Amanda LeVine, 2002

"My favorite aspect of the course, and of geography as a whole, is the visual presentation of information on maps. The ability to learn so much about a subject in such a short amount of time is rarely equaled in any other subject matter. The class also looked at issues from both sides, giving a fair chance to every idea we were taught about. Because of my experiences in AP Human Geography I became interested in Urban and Economical geography and how the two are connected. I am now pursuing a career in urban and regional planning. The class is practical for anyone looking to become more open minded and culturally sensitive. The class was the most influential and informative class I took while in high school." —Ben Lykins, 2010

"AP Human Geo forced me to consider fundamental questions about the human condition as it plays out, and has played out, in societies around the world. These questions led me to study Sociology in college, where I constantly drew upon lessons from the class, not to mention the demographic transition model coming up in conversation at a restaurant last week—true story."

—Carl Johnson, 2004

"I learned more about the world in AP Human Geography than in any other history class I have ever taken. It allowed me to gain a better understanding of the relationships between various countries and the impacts they have on a global level."   —Meghna Murali, 2009

"Human geography, contrary to my first impression, was much more than JUST geography. I learned about different ways of life, and it allowed me to see the world in a whole new way. Let's just say that from the beginning to the end of my sophomore year, it wasn't the world that changed, but my increased interest and awareness of 'the why of where' that changed my perspective. Now I can't even go to the mall without thinking about globalization!"

—Sammi Roth, 2011

"Human Geography changed my life! Yes, I know it sounds cliché but this course has the potential to make a huge impact on the lives of its students. Going into the course, I had a very narrow world view. I was unconcerned with other cultures and even more oblivious to the effect that they had on my life without me even realizing Geography exposed me to unique concepts that I now enjoy finding in day to day life. More than anything, Human Geography changed my future. I had always had a love for politics, but this course helped me discover that it's not the politics I love, but more the people who determine them. Who will vote for which candidate? How can I court a new voter population? Where are the voters? All of these questions and more were answered within my Human Geography course and for that reason I now want to become a political strategist. This course is an exhilarating combination of math, science, history, even literature, there is literally something for everyone and I would highly encourage anyone and everyone to take this course."

—Rachel Harris, 2012

SECTION 3
WHAT DOES THE "AP" MEAN IN AP HUMAN GEOGRAPHY? ALL ABOUT THE COLLEGE BOARD AND ADVANCED PLACEMENT PROGRAM

The purpose of this section is to have you understand what AP Human Geography is and how the program works. We've developed three sections to help you get a strong understanding of the program:

A.   What Are the Most Frequently Asked Questions about the Program?
B.   What Are the Topics Covered in AP Human Geography?
C.   What Are Some Tips for Taking an AP Human Geography Test?

A. What Are the Most Frequently Asked Questions about the Program?

In Part A, we will attempt to answer some of the most frequently asked questions about the Advanced Placement Program and AP Human Geography specifically.

What is the Advanced Placement (AP) program?

AP stands for Advanced Placement and it is a program of college-level courses and exams that gives high school students the opportunity to receive advanced placement and/or credit from the college they attend. The courses that AP offers reflect the content and goals of a first-year college course that is offered by a large number of colleges and universities.

The Advanced Placement Program is administered and managed by the College Board, the same organization that offers the SAT each year.

How can a student participate in Advanced Placement?

Typically students take a class with a teacher who has been approved by the College Board. Teachers of Advanced Placement courses must submit a course syllabus to ensure that what they are teaching matches up with the expectations of a college-level course.

Sometimes students will take the course on their own through an online course, independent study, or tutor.

Whatever the case may be, students have the chance to take an AP exam for the course they selected at the end of the year. Every May, over 1 million exams are administered to high school students throughout the world. Please go to collegeboard.com for more information about all the 34 different courses offered in the Advanced Placement program.

How many students are involved in the AP Human Geography program?

AP® Human Geography: By the Numbers—History of the Exam

YEAR	# of Exams	% Change	# Schools
2001	3,272	-	305
2002	5,286	62	402
2003	7,329	39	473
2004	10,471	43	561
2005	14,139	35	702
2006	21,003	38	890
2007	29,005	49	1,083
2008	39,878	37	1,380
2009	50,730	27	1,618
2010	68,397	35	1,951
2011	83,086	21	Data not available
2012	*97,000	Data not available	Data not available

Projected numbers as of June 2012.
Source: Barbara Hildebrant—Educational Testing Service, Personal Communication to Paul Gray (email), May 30, 2012.

What is the format of the AP Human Geography exam?

The AP Human Geography exam lasts 2 hours and 15 minutes.

It contains two sections:

1. 75 Multiple Choice Questions (MCQs)
2. 3 Free Response Questions (FRQs)

Both portions of the test are worth 50% of a student's grade.

Students have 1 hour to finish the Multiple Choice section. Then, after a short break, they have 75 minutes to answer three Free Response Questions (each FRQ averages 25 minutes).

How are the exams scored?

Multiple Choice Questions are machine scored.

Free Response Questions are more complicated. They are scored by a large number of college geography professors and Advanced Placement Human Geography teachers who meet together during the first weeks in June. These professors and teachers work in groups and focus on one of the questions using a standard rubric. Team leaders do frequent cross checks to assure validity and consistency in grading.

Each exam receives a final score based on a five-point scale:

5   Extremely well qualified

4   Well qualified

3   Qualified

2   Possibly qualified

1   No recommendation

How can I earn college credit and placement?

According to the College Board website, more than 90% of four-year colleges in the United States and colleges in more than 60 other countries give students credit, advanced placement, or both, on the basis of AP exam scores.

Each college and university sets its own policies on what scores, if any, it will accept for credit and/or advanced placement. But you can go to the College Board website or http://collegesearch. collegeboard.com/apcreditpolicy/index.jsp for more specific information.

Searching the above site in 2011, we came up with a sampling of a few universities' policies. The summaries are as follows.

Florida State University (Tallahassee, Florida)

Students who have participated in the AP Program in high school and received a score of 3 or better on the national examinations will receive college credit in the appropriate subject areas. Please refer to our website for information about specific scores and credits.

University of Idaho (Moscow, Idaho)

Credit is granted for Advanced Placement courses completed in high school in which a grade of 5, 4, or 3 is attained in College Board Advanced Placement exams.

Clemson University (Clemson, South Carolina)

Clemson University credit is awarded for grades of 3, 4, or 5 on AP exams.

Drake University (Des Moines, Iowa)

Drake University encourages students to enroll in Advanced Placement courses. Students in AP courses have been more successful in gaining admission to Drake because they are well prepared. Drake University awards advanced standing credit through several programs. In consultation with faculty advisers, all credits accepted are applied toward completion of Drake Curriculum, major, or elective requirements.

In addition to these blurbs, there are links to the college's website for even more specific detail.

(All four of these colleges accept AP Human Geography credit with a score of 3 or higher except Drake University, which accepts a score of 4 or higher.)

How much does it cost to take the Advanced Placement Human Geography exam?

As of 2011, the fee for each exam is $87.

Also as of 2011, some states pay all fees for students to take AP exams.

To encourage AP access and equity, most states offer discounted fees for students whose families may not be able to afford the cost of the AP exam.   Check with your high school counselor or AP teacher for more information as to if you qualify for reduced exam fees. The fee for exams administered at schools outside of the United States, U.S. territories and commonwealths, and Canada, with the exception of U.S. Department of Defense Dependents Schools (DoDDS), is $117 per exam.

The fee for exams administered at College Board-authorized testing centers outside of the United States is $143 per exam.[1]

Obviously, we are extremely sensitive to the fact that $87 or more is a lot of money for many families. We encourage students whose families have financial need to go to the College Board website and find out about fee reductions for those in financial need.[7]

Visit   http://professionals.collegeboard.com/testing/ap/coordinate/fee-assistance/state   for more details on state assistance.

Should I take the Advanced Placement exam?

This is a question we get a lot. To best answer the question, we need to start with a new one, "Why would you NOT take the AP exam?" After all, being in the course all year and not taking the exam is like going to basketball practices all year and never playing in the game.

Here are some facts:

1.   By taking a college-level exam, you get a great sense of what it feels like to be in college and how prepared you are among your peers.
2.   By taking a challenging exam, you are pushing yourself to become smarter.
3.   A low score doesn't hurt your G.P.A at your school. A high score can you can get college credit for less than $100! Sweet!
4.   A high score might get you into that tough college (see the admissions statement from Drake University).

Taking the AP Human Geography exam could be one of the best investments you can make. College courses cost thousands of dollars. According to the College Board, many students who have done well on several AP exams can actually finish college in 3 years or complete a double-major in four years.

Our advice is, as long as money isn't the issue, take the exam and grow from the experience.

---

[7] http://www.collegeboard.com/student/testing/ap/cal_fees.html

When will I find out my score?

AP scores are sent out by the College Board in July (usually in the second week) and are free of charge. If you are anxious and would like to get your score earlier, the College Board provides a phone service starting on July 1 that gives you your score by phone for $8. The phone numbers for that service are:

- 1-888-308-0013 (toll free in the United States, U.S. territories, and Canada)
- 1-609-771-7366 (outside of the United States, U.S. territories, and Canada)

More information about scores (and canceling poor scores) is available on the College Board website. You can go directly to this link:

http://www.collegeboard.com/student/testing/ap/exgrd_rep.html

What if I have more questions about the AP exam?

The best resources for you are the College Board website and the AP coordinator at your school. Every school should have an administrator in charge of Advanced Placement. Those individuals will have detailed information specific to each school. It is not a bad idea for you to find out who that person is as early as possible—just in case. Your teacher should be able to tell you who is the AP coordinator for your school or district.

How should I prepare for the exam?

We will provide you some basic test tips in this section. In addition, at the end of this study guide, there is plenty of advice on how to prepare for the AP exam and a practice AP exam for you to take.

B. What Are the Topics Covered in AP Human Geography?

Part B is designed to get you into the mindset of the College Board and those who designed the course and the test. We really want you to understand the key concepts and ideas this course addresses.

1. Course Description

The MOST IMPORTANT information about the AP Human Geography exam and how to prepare for the course is in a small booklet called *AP Human Geography: Course Description* published by the College Board. You can download it free at:

http://www.collegeboard.com/student/testing/ap/sub_humangeo.html?humangeo

OR you can simply search the web for "AP Human Geography Course Description" and the PDF should be available for you.

Now, why is this the MOST IMPORTANT information about the AP exam? Simply put, the people who created this booklet create the exam! So, in essence it is the closest you will get to understanding what the "AP Gods" are thinking. There are even practice questions in the booklet.

We will give you a glimpse into that booklet and the thinking in the sections below.

2.   *The Five Major Goals of AP Human Geography*

The people who designed the AP Human Geography exam based the content on *five college-level goals* that build on the National Geography Standards. These five goals truly describe what this course is about and what skills you should acquire after completing the class. As the booklet points out, if you successfully complete the course and do well on the exam, you should be able to do the following:

Use and think about maps and spatial data.

Geography is concerned with the ways in which patterns on Earth's surface reflect and influence physical and human processes. As such, maps and spatial data are fundamental to the discipline, and learning to use and think about them is critical to geographical literacy. The goal is achieved when students learn to use maps and spatial data to pose and solve problems, and when they learn to think critically about what is revealed and what is hidden in different maps and spatial arrays.

Understand and interpret the implications of associations among phenomena in places.

Geography looks at the world from a spatial perspective, seeking to understand the changing spatial organization and material character of Earth's surface. One of the critical advantages of a spatial perspective is the attention it focuses on how phenomena are related to one another in particular places. Students should thus learn not just to recognize and interpret patterns but to assess the nature and significance of the relationships among phenomena that occur in the same place, and to understand how tastes and values, political regulations, and economic constraints work together to create particular types of cultural landscapes.

Recognize and interpret at different scales the relationships among patterns and processes.

Geographical analysis requires a sensitivity to scale, not just as a spatial category but as a framework for understanding how events and processes at different scales influence one another. Thus, students should understand that the phenomena they are studying at one scale (e.g., local) may well be influenced by developments at other scales (e.g., regional, national, or global). They should then look at processes operating at multiple scales when seeking explanations of geographic patterns and arrangements.

Define regions and evaluate the regionalization process.

Geography is concerned not simply with describing patterns but with analyzing how they came about and what they mean. Students should see regions as objects of analysis and exploration and move beyond simply locating and describing regions to considering how and why they come into being and what they reveal about the changing character of the world in which we live.

Characterize and analyze changing interconnections among places.

At the heart of a geographical perspective is a concern with the ways in which events and processes operating in one place can influence those operating at other places. Thus, students should view places and patterns not in isolation but in terms of their spatial and functional relationship with other places and patterns. Moreover, they should strive to be aware that those relationships are constantly changing, and they should understand how and why change occurs.

3. Topics in AP Human Geography

AP Human Geography covers seven major topics throughout the year. The following lists the topics in the order assigned by the College Board (please note that teachers sometimes will cover these topics in a different order):

Content Area (Topic)	_Percentage Goals for Exam_
I. Geography: Its Nature and Perspectives	5–10%
II. Population	13–17%
III. Cultural Patterns and Processes	13–17%
IV. Political Organization of Space	13–17%
V. Agriculture and Rural Land Use	13–17%
VI. Industrialization and Economic Development	13–17%
VII. Cities and Urban Land Use	13–17%

The percentages mark the range of multiple choice questions that will be on the AP exam from each section.

To help you to better understand what these topics are, the AP Human Geography Course Description gives brief summaries of the units. We have included those summaries and the complete AP Human Geography Topic Outline in Part 3 of this book: *How to Prepare for the AP Human Geography Exam.* When you are ready to begin studying for the AP exam, please go to this section of the book for valuable information.

C. What Are Some Tips for Taking Tests in Your AP Human Geography Course?

If you are looking for some tips on how to answer Multiple Choice Questions and Free Response Questions throughout the school year, we suggest you jump to Part 3 of this book. Part 3 is a review of the AP exam, and the three sections are as follows:

- Review of Multiple Choice Questions
- Review of Free Response Questions
- Practice Exams

We realize that most AP Human Geography teachers will give you Multiple Choice Questions and Free Response Questions like the samples found in Part 3. You might therefore want to look at Part 3 at the beginning of the year and then again as you prepare for the AP Human Geography exam throughout the school year.

PART 2:
UNDERSTANDING YOUR TEXTBOOK

SECTION 1
HOW TO READ YOUR TEXTBOOK:
TOOLS YOU CAN USE WHEN YOU READ

> The purpose of this section is to teach you how to read your *Human Geography: People, Place, and Culture* textbook. There are three parts to this section:
> A. Learning to Read Again: RUS (Are You Serious)?
> B. How Is a Chapter Designed?
> C. Tools for Each Chapter

A. Learning to Read Again: RUS (Are You Serious)?

Yes, you know how to read. But let's face it, these days for many of you it comes in the form of text messages—AYK (as you know). A whole language and skill are involved in being able to read text messages. In fact, you developed that skill over time. However, thanks to your parents' generous cell phone plan and several crises at school, you worked and developed that skill and became better at writing and reading text messages. Who knew that texting was a skill? LOL (laugh out loud).

And much like understanding how to decode text messages is a skill, learning how to read a college-level geography text is something that will take some time getting used to. OMG!

Seriously, for many of you, this is your first Advanced Placement course. Taking a college-level course requires understanding a very comprehensive and often nuanced vocabulary.

> Translation for you: There are a lot of big words that you might be unfamiliar with, and there are sometimes similar words that have slightly different meanings.

In addition, this might be your first geography class or perhaps your last geography class was in elementary school. So, you are probably unfamiliar with geographic thinking; therefore, reading a geography book will be challenging.

The rest of this section is accordingly set up to help you become a more skilled reader of your textbook. We will go through the format of each chapter. We will also give you reading tools that we have created that force you to be a more careful reader. Our hope is that you read this material BEFORE you start your textbook, so that you will begin the year on the right foot. We believe that by the end of the year you probably won't need to use every tool because you will have trained yourself to do it instinctively.

Remember, we're JHO and this is FYI. You could DIY, but you probably would FDGB!

Translation for your teacher: Remember, we're <u>just helping out</u> and this is <u>for your information</u>. You could <u>do it yourself</u>, but you probably would <u>fall down—go boom</u>.

B. How Is a Chapter Designed?

The best way to prepare to read your textbook is to have an idea of how each chapter is designed. Your textbook has a wonderful format, and once you get a feel for it, the better you will anticipate what is coming up next and make better connections.

Here is the basic structure of every chapter:

1. Field Note

The introduction to the chapter comes in the form of a wonderful primary source account. One of the three authors reflects on a place he or she has studied and connects it to what you will be studying. Through pictures and vivid descriptions of a particular location, you are transported to that location (without ever leaving home). Typically, once a particular location is described, the scale is changed and the focus becomes more global. Sometimes maps are included to give you additional data to help you better understand.

The purpose is to hopefully create excitement and interest, but at the very least to provide a "discussion-style" reading for you—to give you the feel that the author is talking just to you. Sure, sometimes big vocabulary words are used in the Field Note, but generally the idea is to give you a sense of place and a sense of the importance of the chapter you are going to begin.

We often find that students will only glance through the Field Note. We feel this is not only unfortunate, but unwise.

2. Key Questions List

After the Field Note, the next part of the chapter presents a list of Key Questions. The Key Questions are actually the titles to the sections of the chapter and there are typically four or five in every chapter.

We creatively offer you these sections in the form of a question because the question should immediately trigger to you what you are about to read. For instance in Chapter 2, one of the Key Questions is "Why do people migrate?" Well, if you don't know why people migrate, you should know a lot about it by the end of the section.

We also like to list all the Key Questions right after the Field Note. This should give you a greater understanding of the overall goals of the chapter.

Again, we think many students glance through these Key Questions without giving them much thought.

3. A Key Question

In the next part of a chapter you specifically begin to read a specific section (Key Question). You need to understand a few things before you begin reading a Key Question. For starters, not all Key Questions are the same length. So it is important to look at the length of the section before you begin reading. This will better prepare you for how long you will need to focus.

The other things you need to know are as follow:

- *Key Questions* are denoted in **BOLD** and are set in ALL CAPS.
- *Subsections* within the Key Question are denoted in **green and in boldface.** Subsections are typically 4 to 10 paragraphs long.
- Key terms (which are called *Geographic Concepts*) will be in **bold** as you read. Please note that you should be able to understand a Geographic Concept within the context of the reading. However, if you are unable to do so, you can go to the glossary in the Appendix of the book for a full definition.
- Each Key Question ends with a *Thinking Geographically* feature. Typically, this feature gets you to consider your own world and geography. It also encourages you to think about geography in your space.

4. Maps, Photos, Charts, and Graphs

Throughout every chapter there are a series of photographs, maps, charts, and graphs. All of these visual aids are extremely important. We know that in other textbooks many of you see a picture or map and go "Hooray!" Your thought is that you can skip over the visual and therefore have less to read. But remember, geography is a spatial class and is therefore one in which being a visual learner is important.

All of the visuals contain information that is important and can be assessed on a test. A picture can really give you a sense of place, a sense of the human element in geography. Right now, imagine you are in India. What would that picture look like? That picture could be different for all of us depending on where we are in India: near a sacred site, in downtown Bangalore, or in a rural rice village. However, those images are filled with an imprint of technology, culture, and human interaction with the environment. And they differ throughout the world.

Charts and graphs do a great job of presenting data to you in a visual way making it easy to compare and contrast information. For instance, in your textbook on p. 61, there are Age–Sex Population Pyramids for poorer countries and for wealthier countries. These images do a great job of visually demonstrating the contrast in these countries' populations.

Maps are probably the most essential visual used in the textbook. In fact, Appendix A in your textbook gives you a crash course on the importance of maps. It is something we encourage you to read at the beginning of the year.

And while maps are important in a geography class, world maps are the kings. Every chapter in your textbook has at least one world map (Chapter 1 has four). World maps are the cool kid in class, the smart kid in school, the best musician in the band, and the varsity athlete all rolled into one. And of course, they are very attractive.

And whether it is love at first sight or a gradual process of getting to know the world maps and learning to appreciate them, you will become attached to them.

At the same time, we are aware that this might be your first time having to read a map for deep meaning. We also know that you might look at a map for a while and think you've learned the information, but you might have missed a portion of the information.

5. Guest Field Note

Occasionally, a picture will be accompanied by another Field Note. Just like the Field Note at the beginning of the chapter, this field note is a snapshot of a particular place. Again, it gives you another opportunity to see the application of a concept in the real world. You should always include these additional Field Notes in your notes.

6. Summary

Each chapter concludes with a summary. This is truly a great way to make sure you have understood the overarching framework of the chapter. If you read the summary and are confused, then you need to go back and reread the chapter. And even if you understand the summary, that does not guarantee you success on a test. Remember, the summary is a framework or a general understanding of the chapter. In a college-level course, details are going to be key.

We believe that if you've taken notes throughout the chapter then the summary should make sense. We also believe that you will have enough detail in your notes to do well on tests.

7. Geographic Concepts

One of the last parts of the chapter is a list of all the key vocabulary terms that you need to know. These were all the bold words in your textbook, and there are definitions for all of these words in your glossary. It is probably a good idea to look at this list after studying and see if you can recall the term without looking up the definition. If you can, you've got it! If not, you need to go to your notes, reread the definition, or go back to the text.

8. Learn More Online and Watch It Online

The final part of the chapter gives you an opportunity to explore the geographic topic on your own and in more detail. Specific websites are given to you for further research.

C. Tools for Each Chapter

Okay, now you know the format for each chapter. We have created "The Five Steps to Chapter Success" for each chapter. We believe that if you follow these steps, you will have a much better understanding and a better chance for success on the tests.

The Five Steps to Chapter Success

> Step 1: Read the Chapter Summary below, preview the Key Questions, the Chapter Outline, and the Geographic Concepts.
>
> Step 2: Complete the Pre-Reading Activity (PRA) for this chapter.
>
> Step 3: Read the chapter and complete the guided worksheet.
>
> Step 4: As you read the chapter, complete World Regions Map Sheets for every world map. Go to the Student Companion Website to print out the WRMS.
>
> Step 5: Take a Practice AP-style practice quiz.

As you get into each chapter, the steps should be pretty clear. However, since this is a geography class, Step 4 is a VERY IMPORTANT STEP that will help you improve your reading of maps and your understanding of geography.

World Regions Map Sheet (WRMS): The Purpose of Step 4

The purpose of the World Regions Map Sheet (WRMS) is to make sure you are reading the maps for detail. It is very important skill for a geography class.

World maps are like elephants. They're big, tough, and hard to sink your teeth into—not that you would want to eat an elephant. But think for a second, what if you had to eat an elephant? How would you do it? Hopefully, you would consider going slowly and eating it bit by bit.

Staring at a world map can be as overwhelming as thinking about consuming a whole elephant. The trick with both is to consume a map piece by piece instead of swallowing it whole.

When you see a world map on population, it's easy to pick up overall information, just like it's easy to see that an elephant is gray. But the trick of learning how to read a world map effectively is learning how to divide it into parts and finding patterns on a smaller scale. In essence, it amounts to "eating" the map bit by bit.

The WRMS are designed to help you read (consume) the maps effectively. WRM Sheets divide the world into 11 different regions based on human/cultural elements. These regions are as follows:

1. North America
2. Latin America (Middle America, Caribbean, and South America)
3. Europe

4. North Africa and Southwest Asia

5. Subsaharan Africa

6. Russia (with Armenia, Azerbaijan, and Georgia)

7. South Asia

8   East Asia

9. Southeast Asia

10. Austral (Australia, New Zealand)

11. South Pacific Islands

Figure 2.1 shows you where these regions are in the world.

We have also provided you with a list of the major countries from each of these regions (see page 33). You will see these countries on the world maps used in your textbook. Small countries (microstates) such as Andorra or Seycelles are not included in this list due to their small scale, but the country list includes the major countries in the world.

There are a few things to note about the regions we have created:

- These regions reflect the *human* or cultural elements of geography rather than physical elements (otherwise Mexico would be included in the North American Region). Mexico's language, religion, and culture tie it to Latin America despite its being a physical part of North America.

- These are perceptual regions meaning different people might define these regions differently depending on varying characteristics. You'll learn about this in Chapter 1 in your textbook.

On page 35, we have provided you with a sample of a WRMS. This sheet should be filled out every time you read a world map in your textbook. Additional WRMS are on the Student Companion Website and are available for you to download and print.

The WRMS includes a list of each region and space in between so that you can take notes. There are additional prompts that give you an opportunity to comment on patterns you see. These sheets should help you take the time to read world maps slowly and effectively.

Just remember: you need to look at a map from both a general and a specific perspective. You need to search for patterns. And do remember **where** and **why**! When you take notes on a map, think about the following:

- Where is "it" occurring?

- Where is "it" not occurring?

- Is there a pattern?

- Why is there a pattern?

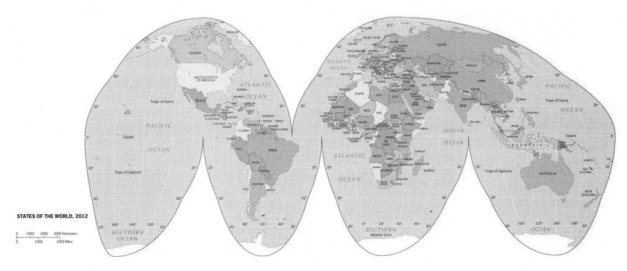

HUMAN GEOGRAPHY: WORLD REGION MAPS

Below is a list of the major countries located in the 11 world regions on a world map.

1   North America

Canada   United States

2   Latin America (Middle America, Caribbean, and South America)

Argentina	Belize	Bolivia	Brazil
Chile	Colombia	Costa Rica	Cuba
Dominican Republic	Ecuador	El Salvador	French Guiana
Guatemala	Guyana	Haiti	Honduras
Jamaica	Mexico	Nicaragua	Panama
Paraguay	Peru	Puerto Rico (U.S.)	Suriname
Uruguay	Venezuela		

3   Europe

Albania	Austria	Belarus	Belgium
Bosnia and Herzegovina	Bulgaria	Croatia	Czech Republic
Denmark	Estonia	Finland	France
Germany	Greece	Hungary	Iceland
Ireland	Italy	Kosovo	Latvia
Liechtenstein	Lithuania	Luxembourg	Macedonia
Malta	Moldova	Montenegro	Netherlands
Norway	Poland	Portugal	Romania
Serbia	Slovakia	Slovenia	Spain
Sweden	Switzerland	Ukraine	United Kingdom

4   North Africa and Southwest Asia

Afghanistan	Algeria	Bahrain	Egypt
Iran	Iraq	Israel	Jordan
Kazakhstan	Kuwait	Kyrgyzstan	Lebanon
Libya	Morocco	Oman	Qatar
Saudi Arabia	Sudan	Syria	Tajikistan
Tunisia	Turkey	Turkmenistan	
United Arab Emirates	Uzbekistan	Western Sahara	Yemen

5   Subsaharan Africa

Angola	Benin	Botswana	Burkina Faso
Burundi	Cameroon	Central African	Republic
Chad	Congo	Comoros	Dem. Rep. of Congo
Djibouti	Equatorial Guinea	Eritrea	Ethiopia
Gabon	Gambia	Ghana	Guinea
Guinea-Bissau	Ivory Coast	Kenya	Lesotho
Liberia	Madagascar	Malawi	Mali
Mauritius	Mozambique	Namibia	Niger
Nigeria	Rwanda	Senegal	Sierra Leone
Somalia	South Africa	South Sudan	Swaziland
Tanzania	Togo	Uganda	Zambia
Zimbabwe			

6   Russia and Caucasus states

Russia	Armenia	Azerbaijan	Georgia

7   South Asia

Bangladesh	India	Pakistan	Sri Lanka
Bhutan	Nepal		

8   East Asia

China	Mongolia	North Korea	South Korea
Japan	North Korea	Taiwan (PRC)	

9   Southeast Asia

Brunei	Cambodia	East Timor	Indonesia
Laos	Malaysia	Myanmar (Burma)	Philippines
Singapore	Thailand	Vietnam	

10   South Pacific

Fiji	New Caledonia	Papua New Guinea
Solomon Islands	Vanuati	

11   Austral Region

Australia   New Zealand

The following is a sample of a World Region Mapping Sheet (WRMS), which you should complete every time you see a map. Additional WRMS's are available on the student companion website.

WORLD REGION MAPPING SHEET (WRMS)

Student Name _____   **Chapter** _____

Title (Map): _____   **pages** _____

Think Spatially: Look at the map and find patterns that seem to exist in general.

List five general facts/patterns found on this map:

1. _____
   _____
2. _____
   _____
3. _____
   _____
4. _____
   _____
5. _____
   _____

Think Regionally: Now, focus on a particular region and list key details from the map for each region (bullet points are fine).

1.   North America

2.   Latin America (Middle America, Caribbean, and South America)

3.   Europe

4.   North Africa and Southwest Asia

5.   Subsaharan Africa

6.   Russia (with Armenia, Azerbaijan and Georgia)

7.   South Asia

8.   East Asia

9.   Southeast Asia

10.   South Pacific Islands

11.   Austral (Australia, New Zealand)

SECTION 2:
CHAPTER PREP

CHAPTER 1:
INTRODUCTION TO HUMAN GEOGRAPHY

The Five Steps to Chapter Success

Step 1: Read the Chapter Summary below, preview the Key Questions, the Chapter Outline, and
      Geographic Concepts.

Step 2: Complete the Pre-Reading Activity (PRA) for this chapter.

Step 3: Read the chapter and complete the guided worksheet.

Step 4: As you read the chapter, complete World Region Map Sheets for every world map.
      Go to the Student Companion Website to print out the WMRS.

Step 5: Take a Practice AP-style practice quiz.

STEP 1: Chapter Summary, Key Questions, Chapter Outline, and Geographic Concepts

Chapter Summary

Our study of human geography will analyze people and places and explain how they interact across space and time to create our world. Chapters 2 and 3 lay the basis for our study of human geography by looking at where people live. Chapters 4–7 focus on aspects of culture and how people use culture and identity to make sense of themselves in their world. The remaining chapters examine how people have created a world in which they function economically, politically, and socially, and how their activities in those realms re-create themselves and their world.

Key Questions

Field Note: Awakening to World Hunger	1–8
1. What is human geography?	8–9
2. What are geographic questions?	9–15
3. Why do geographers use maps, and what do maps tell us?	15–22
4. Why are geographers concerned with scale and connectedness?	23–31
5. What are geographic concepts, and how are they used in answering geographic questions?	32–33

Chapter 1 Outline

A. What Is Human Geography?
B. What Are Geographic Questions?
    1. Introduction
    2. Maps in the Time of Cholera Pandemics
    3. The Spatial Perspective
        a. The Five Themes
        b. Cultural Landscape
C. Why Do Geographers Use Maps, and What Do Maps Tell Us?
    1. Introduction
    2. Mental Maps
    3. Generalization in Maps
D. Remote Sensing and GISD. Why Are Geographers Concerned with Scale and
    Connectedness?
    1. Introduction
    2. Regions
        a. Introduction: Formal, Functional, and Perceptual
        b. Perceptual Regions in the United States
    3. Culture
    4. Connectedness through Diffusion
        a. Introduction
        b. Expansion Diffusion
        c. Relocation Diffusion
E. What Are Geographic Concepts, and How Are They Used in Answering Geographic
    Questions?
    1. Introduction
    2. Environmental Determinism
    3. Possibilism
    4. Today's Human Geography

Geographic Concepts		
Fieldwork	Spatial Interaction	Formal/Perceptual Region
Human Geography	Distance	Culture
Globalization	Accessibility	Culture Trait
Physical Geography	Connectivity	Culture Complex
Spatial	Landscape	Cultural Hearth
Spatial Distribution	Cultural Landscape	Independent Invention
Pattern	Sequent Occupance	Cultural Diffusion
Medical Geography	Cartography	Time-Distance Decay

Pandemic	Reference Maps	Cultural Barrier
Epidemic	Thematic Maps	Expansion Diffusion
Spatial Perspective	Absolute Location	Contagious Diffusion
Five Themes	Global Positioning System	Hierarchical Diffusion
Location	Geocaching	Stimulus Diffusion
Location Theory	Relative Location	Relocation Diffusion
Human–Environment	Mental Map	Geographic Concept
Region	Activity Space	Environmental Determinism
Place	Generalized Map	Possibilism
Sense of Place	Remote Sensing	Cultural Ecology
Perception of Place	Geographic Information Systems	Political Ecology
Movement	Rescale	

Step 2: Pre-Reading Activity (PRA)

Name: _____ **Period** _____ **Date** _____

Chapter Title: _____

Chapter # _____   **Pgs.** _____ **to** _____

1. Write down each of the Key Questions and the number of pages for each (go back to Step 1 of your textbook for answers).

Key Question	# of Pages

2. After looking over the Key Questions, looking through the outline, and reading the chapter summary, write a few sentences about what you expect to learn in general in this chapter.

3.   Preview the entire chapter and look at all the maps, tables, charts, and pictures. Read the captions. Briefly describe IN YOUR OWN WORDS five maps or charts.

pg. _____ _____

pg. _____ _____

pg. _____ _____

pg. _____ _____

pg. _____ _____

4.   How many world maps are there in this chapter? _____ (Go to the Student Companion Website and print out the World Map Region Worksheets needed for this chapter.)

5.   Read the Field Note introduction of the chapter and list five specific facts you learned.

_____

_____

_____

_____

_____

_____

_____

_____

_____

_____

_____

6.   Go to Step 1 and look at the Geographic Concepts. Create a list of terms you think you know and terms you need to know.

I THINK I KNOW	I NEED TO LEARN

Step 3: Chapter 1 Guided Worksheet (Created by Parisa Watson)

Name: _____ Period _____ Date_____

Directions: As you read the chapter, fill in the blanks on the guided worksheet.

FIELD NOTE—AWAKENING TO WORLD HUNGER

1. Much of Kenya's income comes from _Coffee_ and _Tea_ production.
2. It is estimated that even today, _one seventh_ of the world's population is malnourished.
3. The vast majority of the _one billion_ malnourished people on Earth are women and _Children_, who have little _money_ and even less _power_.

WHAT IS HUMAN GEOGRAPHY?

4. Human geographers study _people_ and places. The field of _human geography_ focuses on how people make places, how we organize space and society, how we interact with each other in places and across space, and how we make sense of others and ourselves in our localities, regions and the world.
5. Advances in communication and _transportation_ _technologies_ are making places and people more _interconnected_. (Steamship, the railroad, and the horse, and buggy.
6. The set of processes that are increasing interactions, heightening interdependence, and depending relationships is called _Globalization._

WHAT ARE GEOGRAPHIC QUESTIONS?

7. While human geography is the study of the spatial and material characteristics of human places and people found on the Earth's surface, _physical geography_ asks similar questions about the natural environment. Mikesell once gave a shorthand definition of geography as the "_Why_ of _where_."
8. Geographers interest in the arrangement of places and phenomena, including its layout is known as the _spatial_ perspective.
9. Cholera is an example of a _pandemics_, or worldwide outbreak of a disease. _Dr. Snow_ found the source of cholera in London's water pumps.
10. While cholera has not been completely defeated, people now know that cholera can be contacted by eating food or contaminated _water_ with cholera bacteria.
11. An _epidemic_ disease is a regional outbreak of a disease.
12. The five themes of geography are: _Location, human enviomment, region, place and movement._
13. Studying the impact of the drainage of part of the Florida Everglades would focus on the theme of _human and enviroment_.
14. Infusing a place with meaning and emotion gives it a _sense_ of _place_.
15. Our perception of place is influenced by _books, movies, stories and pictures_. In a student survey, responses indicated that there was a strong bias for their _home region_.

Geographer victoria Lawson uses the term jumping
scale to describe such rescaling activities.

16. The degree of linkage between locations in a network is called _connectivity._ .

17. _Sequent occuponce_ refers to the imprints of occupants, whose impacts are _layered_ one on top of the other, each layer having some impacts on the next. (Tanzian city of Dar es Salaam)

18. The _Cultural landscape_ is a term coined by Carl Sauer and refers to the visible imprint of human activity on the landscape.

WHY DO GEOGRAPHERS USE MAPS, AND WHAT DO MAPS TELL US?

19. Map making is known as _Cartography_. Absolute location involves using both _Reference maps_ and _Coordinate system_ to know the exact spot of a place.

20. _Relative location_ describes the location of a place in relation to other human and physical features. *Global positioning system.*

21. _Gps_ allows individuals to locate places on the Earth. It has also created a relatively new hobby called _Geocaching._ .

22. The opening of the St. Lawrence Seaway changed Chicago's _____ _____.

23. A map that we carry in our mind is called a _Mental Maps_. Places we routinely travel in our day are known as our _Activity space_.

24. When geographers monitor the Earth from a distance, it is called _Remote sensing._ .

25. _Gis_ involves maps that have layers that can be added or subtracted to analyze data.
    geographic information system.

WHY ARE GEOGRAPHERS CONCERNED WITH SCALE AND CONNECTEDNESS?

26. Geographers study patterns at a variety of scales: _local_ , _regional_ , _national_ and _global_ .

27. The concern of geography with space puts _rescale_ at the center of its agenda.

28. A _formal_ region is marked by visible uniformity or a shared trait. A _functional_ region involves interactions such as commuting, while a _perceptual region_ is mainly in people's minds.

29. _wilbur Zelinsky_ tackled defining and delimiting perceptual regions in the United States and Canada by analyzing telephone directories.

30. The _____ was the region analyzed that was unlike any of the others.

31. One single attribute of a culture is called a _Cultural trait_. Several aspects of culture combined are called _Culture Complex_ .

32. An area where a culture began is known as a _Cultural hearth_. The spreading of culture is known as _Cultural diffusion_ .

33. The idea that innovations are less accepted the longer it takes to reach its adopters is known as _time distance decay_ .

34. Not all cultural traits or innovations diffuse. Some cultures prohibit the consumption of _alcoholic_ beverages or certain kinds of _meat_ and other foods. Prescriptions cultures make about behavior act as _Cultural barriers_ and can pose powerful obstacles to the spread of ideas or innovations.

35. The two main types of diffusion are _Expansion_ and _Relocation_.
36. Expansion diffusion involves three different types of diffusion: _contagious_, _hierarachial_, and _stimulus_.
37. A type of diffusion where nearly all of the people nearby are affected is _Expansion_.
38. _hierarachial_ diffusion occurs when there is a certain order to who gets what is diffused first, depending on what is diffused (fax machine to offices, Crocs).
39. A third form of expansion diffusion is _stimulus diffusion_. The ____ ____ in India is an example of this type of diffusion.
40. _relocation_ diffusion involves an individual moving and carrying the idea with migrants.

WHAT ARE GEOGRAPHIC CONCEPTS, AND HOW ARE THEY USED IN ANSWERING GEOGRAPHIC QUESTIONS?

41. Huntington and Cushing suggest _Climate_ is the critical factor in how humans behave. _Environmental determinism_ holds that human behavior is affected by the environment, while _possiblism_ argues that nature doesn't control decisions but limits the range of choices.
42. _Cultural ecology_ is concerned with the study of human cultures and their ability to adapt and exist within a particular physical environment. The fundamental doctrine point is that human societies are diverse and the _human_ will is too powerful to be _determined_ by _enviroment_.

Step 4: Remember to fill out World Regions Map Sheets.

Go to the Student Companion Website to print out the sheets: www.wiley.com/college/Fouberg

Step 5: AP-style Practice Quiz

Chapter 1: Introduction to Human Geography

Multiple Choice Questions

1. The vast majority of the 1 billion malnourished people on Earth are
    A. soldiers in countries with insurgencies
    B. people above the age of 65
    C. people with chronic diseases such as HIV/AIDS
    D. women and children
    E. girls under the age of 15

2. Images from a satellite or aerial photos from a plane are both examples of
    A. geographic information systems
    B. map generalization
    C. projection
    D. global positioning
    E. remote sensing

3. A region in which the people share one or more cultural traits is a
    A. functional region
    B. perceptual region
    C. formal region
    D. political region
    E. cultural region

4. A combination of cultural traits is a
    A. complex culture
    B. cultural hearth
    C. barrier to diffusion
    D. culture region
    E. cultural complex

5. Hip-hop culture has spread from city to city worldwide in a process of _____diffusion.
    A. expansion
    B. contagious
    C. stimulus
    D. hierarchical
    E. cultural

6. Latitude and longitude will give you the _____ location of a place.
    A. relative
    B. cultural
    C. reference
    D. situation
    E. absolute

7. All geographers, human or physical, are interested in the _____ of a phenomenon.
    A. spatial distribution
    B. absolute location
    C. diffusion
    D. temporal patterns
    E. origin

8. A set of processes that are increasing interactions and interdependence without regard to country borders is
    A. spatial diffusion
    B. a pandemic
    C. globalization
    D. distance decay
    E. accessibility

9. Which of the following is NOT given as a reason contributing to poverty and malnutrition in Kenya?
    A. a globalized economy that thrives on foreign income
    B. a postcolonial vacuum of well-trained economic managers
    C. tiny farms that are unproductive
    D. a gendered legal system that disenfranchises the agricultural labor force
    E. disempowering of the caregivers of the country's children

10. "From Mannheim Road, go west on North Avenue till you get to 5th Avenue, then north about ¾ of a mile; it's right next to the water tower." This is an example of
    A. relative location
    B. absolute location
    C. the use of GPS
    D. a mental map
    E. geocaching

11. Different Native American populations in the Southwest evolved different forms of economy, some becoming pastoralists, others sedentary farmers, others hunter-gatherers. This can be explained by which geographic concept?
    A. possibilism
    B. environmental determinism
    C. natural isotherms
    D. expansion diffusion
    E. distance decay

12. Why are you not likely to find an all-beef Big Mac at the McDonalds restaurants in India?
    A. chicken is much cheaper to raise in India
    B. most of the people are Hindus who generally do not eat beef
    C. after the last outbreak of mad cow disease, all the cows were slaughtered
    D. all the people of India are vegetarians
    E. lamb is the preferred red meat in South Asia

— Regions, wherefore formal, functional or perceptual are ways of organizing. human geographically,

-They are a form of spatial classification, a means of handling large amount of information, so we can make sense of it.

CHAPTER 2:
POPULATION

The Five Steps to Chapter Success Checklist

Step 1: Read the Chapter Summary below, preview the Key Questions, the Chapter Outline, and the Geographic Concepts of the chapter.

Step 2: Complete the Pre-Reading Activity (PRA) for this chapter.

Step 3: Read the chapter and complete the guided worksheet.

Step 4: As you read the chapter, complete World Region Map Sheets for every world map. Go to the Student Companion Website to print out the WRMS.

Step 5: Take an AP-style Practice Quiz.

STEP 1: Chapter Summary, Key Questions, Chapter Outline, and Geographic Concepts

Chapter Summary

In the late 1700s, Thomas Malthus sounded warning bells about the rapidly growing population in Great Britain. He feared a massive famine would soon "check" the growing population, bringing widespread suffering. Although the famine in Great Britain did not take place as he predicted, the rapidly growing worldwide population made many more follow Malthus's trajectory, issuing similar warnings about the population explosion over the last two centuries.

The growth rate of the world population has certainly slowed, but human suffering is not over yet. Dozens of countries still face high death rates and high birth rates. Even in countries where the death rate is low, slowed population growth is often a result of horrid sanitary and medical conditions that lead to high infant and child mortality, diseases such as AIDS that ravage the population and orphan the young, or famines that governments deny and that global organizations cannot ameliorate.

Population pyramids illustrate that as wealthier countries worry about supporting their aging populations, poorer countries have problems of their own. A high birth rate in a poor country does not necessarily mean overpopulation—some of the highest population densities in the world are found in wealthy countries. Even poor countries that have lowered their birth rates and their death rates are constantly negotiating what is morally acceptable to their people and their cultures.

Geography offers much to the study of population. Through geography we can see differences in population problems across space, how what happens at one scale affects what goes on at other scales, and how different cultures and countries approach population questions.

Key Questions

Chapter 2 Outline

A. Where in the World Do People Live and Why?
   1. Physiologic Population Density
   2. Population Distribution
   3. World Population Distribution and Density
      a. East Asia
      b. South Asia
      c. Europe
      d. North America
   4. Reliability of Population Data
B. Why Do Populations Rise and Fall in Particular Places?
   1. Population Growth at World, Regional, National, and Local Scales
      a. Population at the Regional and National Scales
      b. Population Growth at the Local Scale
   2. The Demographic Transition
   3. Future Population Growth
C. Why Does Population Composition Matter?
D. How Does Geography of Health Influence Population Dynamics?
   1. Infant Mortality
   2. Child Mortality
   3. Life Expectancy
   4. Influence on Health and Well-Being
   5. Infectious Diseases
   6. Chronic and Genetic Diseases
   7. AIDS

E.   How Do Governments Affect Population Change?
1.   Limitations
2.   Contradictions

Geographic Concepts		
Population Density	Population Explosion	Child Mortality Rate
Arithmetic Population Density	Natural Increase	Life Expectancy
	Crude Birth Rate	Infectious Diseases
Physiological Population Density	Crude Death Rate	Chronic or Degenerative Diseases
	Demographic Transition	Genetic or Inherited Diseases
Population Distribution	Stationary Population Level	Endemic AIDS
Dot map	Population Composition	Expansive Population Policies
Megalopolis	Population Pyramids	Eugenic Population Policies
Census	Infant Mortality Rate	Restrictive Population Policies
Doubling Time	Newborn Mortality rate	One-Child Policy

Step 2: Pre-Reading Activity (PRA)

Name: _____ **Period** _____ **Date** _____

Chapter Title: _____

Chapter # _____   **Pgs.** _____ **to** _____

1.   Write down each of the Key Questions and the number of pages for each (go back to Step 1 of your textbook for answers).

Key Question	# of Pages

2.   After looking over the key questions, looking through the outline, and reading the chapter summary, write a few sentences about what you expect to learn in general in this chapter.

3.   Preview the entire chapter and look at all the maps, tables, charts, and pictures. Read the captions. Briefly describe IN YOUR OWN WORDS five maps or charts.

pg. _____ _____

pg. _____ _____

pg. _____ _____

pg. _____ _____

pg. _____ _____

4.   How many world maps are there in this chapter? _____ (Go to the Student Companion Website and print out the World Map Region Worksheets needed for this chapter.)

5.   Read the Field Note introduction of the chapter and list five specific facts you learned.

_____

_____

_____

_____

_____

_____

_____

_____

_____

_____

6.   Go to Step 1 and look at the Geographic Concepts. Create a list of terms you think you know and terms you need to know.

I THINK I KNOW	I NEED TO LEARN

to calculate NIR
subtract- death from births
Imi -out
im -in

52   Part 2   Understanding Your Textbook

Step 3: Chapter 2 Guided Worksheet (Created by Parisa Watson)

Name: _____ **Period** _____ **Date** _____

Directions: As you read the chapter, fill in the blanks on the guided worksheet.

FIELD NOTE—BASIC INFRASTRUCTURE

1. Shanghai now has the longest metro system on Earth—a system capable of transporting 5 million people a day.

2. China's biggest urban challenge may be water as it already has little to spare. 70 % of water use today in China is for agriculture, while demand from urban centers is on the Rise.

WHERE IN THE WORLD DO PEOPLE LIVE AND WHY?

3. Demography is the study of population. Demographers use population density to measure population in relation to land area.

4. Arithmetic population density is the total population of people per unit of land, while physiologic population density is the number of people per unit of arable land. The problem with using Arithmetic population is that it does not take into consideration internal clustering in a country. 98% of Egyptians live on just 3 % of the land.

5. dot maps are commonly used to show population distributions.

6. The three main clusters of population South Asia, East Asia, Europe and a minor concentration of South America Africa North America. The three main clusters are all found on the landmass of Eurasian.

7. A Megalopolis refers to the large cluster of cities close together.

8. In terms of the census, the concern is that people in _____ _____ are undercounted.

WHY DO POPULATIONS RISE OR FALL IN PARTICULAR PLACES?

9. Thomas Malthus believed that the world did not have enough food because he believed food grew Linear while population grew increasing.

10. In general, countries with low population growth are located in wealthy countries.

11. Countries with high population growth are located in US, Europe, Japan, Canada, Australia, New Zealand, uruguay

12. Demographers use total fertility rate (TFR) to measure whether a population can replace its deaths with births. In order to reach replacement levels, this number needs to be 2.1 to keep a stable population. Almost everywhere on Earth, the number is fallen.

13. aging Index is used to compare the population growth rate. In recent years, it has taken _____ time for this to occur.

14. Crude death rate refers to the number of deaths per thousand. Crade birth rate refers to the number of births per thousand.

15. The difference between births and deaths is referred to as the rate of natural increase.

16. The demographic transition model (Figure 2.15) has low growth occurring in stage 1 because of _high_ births and deaths. Stage 2 shows a decrease in the _death_ rate, stage 3 has a population _explosion_. Stage 4 has _decreasing_ growth as both birth and death rates are relatively _low_, while stage 5 marks a population _declining_, with the _birth_ rate falling below the _death_ rate.

WHY DOES POPULATION COMPOSITION MATTER?

17. The number of men and women along with their ages make up the _population composition_ of a country. Geographers use _population pyramid_ to represent these traits visually. They are displayed in percentages of each age group in _5_ year increments by a _horizontal_ bar with _male_ on the left and _female_ on the right.
18. A population pyramid can instantly convey the _demographic situation_ in a country.
19. A population pyramid for a less developed country looks _evergreen tree_ _wide base short ones near top._ while a population pyramid for a more developed country looks like _lopsided vase,_ _____.

HOW DOES THE GEOGRAPHY OF HEALTH INFLUENCE POPULATION DYNAMICS?

20. One of the leading measures of the condition of a country's population is the _infant mortality rate_. It is recorded as a baby's death during the first _year (1-5) age_. Infant and child mortality reflect the overall _health_ of a society.
21. Look at Figure 2.18. In the world, where are infant mortality rates the highest? _Poor countries such Singapore, sweden._
22. Within the United States, where are infant mortality rates the highest? _(second highest newborn death)_ _Alabama, Mississippi and louisana_
23. _life expectancy_ is an indicator of well-being and is higher in more developed countries. They do not take into account _gender_ differences by country. In general, _women_ outlive _men_. Countries such as _Russia_ have a high life expectancy. _(NA, Europe EA)_
24. Diseases can be grouped into categories. 65% of all diseases are _infectious_, resulting from an invasion of parasites and their multiplication in the body. _malaria_ is an infectious disease. The remainder can be divided into _chronic_ or _degenerative_ diseases, the maladies of longevity and old age such as _heart_ disease. _genetic_ or _inherited diseases_ we can trace to our ancestry. _endemic_ is an example of such a disease.
25. There are two types of infectious diseases, _vectored_ and _Nonvectored_. A vectored disease has a _intermediary_ such as the case of malaria with the mosquito.
26. Chronic diseases occur in countries with higher _life_ _expectancies_. Among them, _Heart disease_, _cancer_ and _strokes_ are leading diseases in this category.
27. Low life expectancies in some parts of the world are caused by the ravages of diseases such as _AIDS_. Subsaharan Africa's high mortality rate is strongly influenced by _AIDS_. _____ is reshaping the population structure of the countries hardest hit by the disease.

HOW DO GOVERNMENTS AFFECT POPULATION CHANGE?

28. Over the past century, many of the world's _goverment_ have instituted policies designed to influence the overall _growth_ rate or ethnic ratios within a population. _expansive population policies_ encourage large families. The _Russian_ government offered cash subsidies for women who have 2 or 3 children. Russia's aging population led to a _National day_ of conception.

29. In the past, some governments designed _eugenic population policies_, favoring certain populations over others. _Nazi Germany_ was a drastic example of this policy.

30. Today many of the world's governments seek to reduce the rate of natural increase through various forms of _restrictive population policies_. China's _one child_ policy is an example of such a policy.

Step 4: Remember to fill out World Region Map Sheets.

Go to the Student Companion Website to print out the sheets: www.wiley.com/college/Fouberg

Step 5: Practice Quiz

Chapter 2: Population

Multiple Choice Questions

1. All of the following are components of population growth EXCEPT
    A. crude birth rate
    B. crude death rate
    C. immigration
    D. total fertility rate
    E. emigration

2. An index that relates a country's population density to its available arable land is known as
    A. physiologic density
    B. population density
    C. arithmetic density
    D. distribution density
    E. crop density

3. The region of the world with the largest population density is
    A. Southeast Asia
    B. southern Europe
    C. eastern North America
    D. eastern coastal South America
    E. East Asia

4. According to the text, the world's 2011 population was
    A. 7 million
    B. 10 billion
    C. 9 million
    D. 7 billion
    E. 15 billion

5. Which of the following statements is true?
    A. the slowest growing countries are in the economic core
    B. the slowest growing countries are in the economic periphery
    C. the fastest growing countries are in southern Africa
    D. Russia's population is in decline because of its one-child policy
    E. China's family planning programs once included guns exchanged for sterilization

6. In what two stages of the demographic transition model does population grow rapidly?
    A. stages 1 & 2
    B. stages 2 & 3
    C. stages 3 & 4
    D. stages 1 & 4
    E. stages 4 & 5

7. All of the following are directly indicated on a population pyramid EXCEPT
    A. % of population
    B. life expectancy
    C. age cohorts in five-year increments
    D. males
    E. females

- Child mortality rate - records the death of children between the age 1 to 5.

8. Which of the following countries has the highest life expectancies in the world?
    A. United States
    B. Canada
    C. Sweden
    D. France
    E. Japan

9. Where in the world has the HIV-AIDS epidemic had the greatest impact?
    A. inner-city United States
    B. Russia
    C. Subsaharan Africa
    D. Southeast Asia
    E. Southwest China

10. In countries where cultural traditions restrict educational and professional opportunities for women, and men dominate as a matter of custom, what is the usual impact on population growth rates?
    A. rates of natural increase tend to be high
    B. rates of natural increase tend to be low
    C. total fertility rates tend to be low
    D. infant mortality tends to be high
    E. there is no discernible correlation

CHAPTER 3:
MIGRATION

The Five Steps to Chapter Success

Step 1: Read the Chapter Summary below, preview the Key Questions, the Chapter Outline, and
      the Geographic Concepts of the chapter.
Step 2: Complete the Pre-Reading Activity (PRA) for this chapter.
Step 3: Read the chapter and complete the guided worksheet.
Step 4: As you read the chapter, complete World Region Map Sheets for every world map.
      Go to the Student Companion Website to print out the WMRS.
Step 5: Take an AP-style Practice Quiz.

STEP 1: Chapter Summary, Key Questions, Chapter Outline, and Geographic Concepts

Chapter Summary

In the last 500 years, humans have traveled the globe, mapped it, connected it through globalization, and migrated across it. In this chapter, we discussed major global, regional, and national migration flows. Migration can occur as a result of a conscious decision, resulting in a voluntary migration flow, or migration can occur under duress, resulting in forced migration. Both kinds of migration have left an indelible mark on the world and on its cultural landscapes. Governments attempt to strike a balance among the need for migrant labor, the desire to help people in desperate circumstances, and the desire to stem the tide of migration.

As the world's population mushrooms, the volume of migrants will expand. In an increasingly open and interconnected world, neither physical barriers nor politically motivated legislation will stem tides that are as old as human history. Migrations will also further complicate an already complex global cultural pattern—raising questions about identity, race, ethnicity, language, and religion, the topics we turn to in the next three chapters.

Key Questions

Field Note: Risking Lives for Remittances	78–82
1. What is migration?	82–85
2. Why do people migrate?	85–93
3. Where do people migrate?	93–108
4. How do governments affect migration?	108–110

Chapter 3 Outline

A. What Is Migration?
  1. Cyclic Movement
  2. Periodic Movement
  3. Migration
B. Why Do People Migrate?
  1. Forced Migration
  2. Push and Pull Factors in Voluntary Migration
  3. Types of Push and Pull Factors
    a. Legal Status
    b. Economic Conditions
    c. Power Relationships
    d. Political Circumstances
    e. Armed Conflict and Civil War
    f. Environmental Conditions
    g. Culture and Traditions
    h. Technological Advances
C. Where Do People Migrate?
  1. Global Migration Flows
  2. Regional Migration Flows
    a. Economic Opportunities
    b. Reconnection of Cultural Groups
    c. Conflict and War
  3. National Migration Flows
  4. Guest Workers
  5. Refugees
    a. Regions of Dislocation
D. How Do Governments Affect Migration?
  1. Legal Restrictions
  2. Waves of Immigration in the United States Post-September 11

Geographic Concepts		
Remittances	Voluntary Migration	Colonization
Cyclic Movements	Laws of Migration	Regional Scale
Periodic Movement	Gravity Model	Islands of Development
Migration	Push Factors	Guest Workers
Activity Spaces	Pull Factors	Refugees
Nomadism	Distance Decay	Internally Displaced Persons
Migrant Labor	Step Migration	Asylum
Transhumance	Intervening Opportunity	Repatriation
Military Service	Deportation	Genocide
International Migration	Kinship Links	Immigration Laws
Immigration	Chain Migration	Quotas
Internal Migration	Immigration Wave	Selective Immigration
Forced Migration	Explorers	

Step 2: Pre-Reading Activity (PRA)

Name: _____ **Period** _____   **Date** _____

Chapter Title: _____

Chapter # _____   **Pgs.** _____ **to** _____

1. Write down each of the Key Questions and the number of pages for each (go back to Step 1 or your textbook for answers).

Key Question	# of Pages

2. After looking over the Key Questions and looking through the outline, write a few sentences about what you expect to learn in general in this chapter.

3.   Preview the entire chapter and look at all the maps, tables, charts and pictures. Read the captions. Briefly describe IN YOUR OWN WORDS five maps or charts.

pg. _____ _____

pg. _____ _____

pg. _____ _____

pg. _____ _____

pg. _____ _____

4.   How many world maps are there in this chapter? _____ (Go to the Student Companion Website and print out the World Map Region Worksheets needed for this chapter.)

5.   Read the Field Note introduction of the chapter and list five specific facts you learned.

_____

_____

_____

_____

_____

_____

_____

_____

_____

_____

6.   Go to Step 1 and look at the Geographic Concepts. Create a list of terms you think you know and the terms you need to know.

I THINK I KNOW	I NEED TO LEARN

emigrant subtract from the total population of country.
immigrant adds to the total population of country.

Step 3: Chapter 3 Guided Worksheet (Created by Parisa Watson)

Name: _____ **Period** _____ **Date** _____

Directions: As you read the chapter, fill in the blanks on the guided worksheet.

FIELD NOTE—RISKING LIVES FOR REMITTANCES

1. Immigrants are sometimes welcomed and sometimes _turned_ _away_. In the 1970s, the
    U.S. government welcomed _Haitans_ immigrants because most were _educated_ and able
    to afford _travel_ to the United States.
2. In 1980, _25,000_ _haitan_ and _125,000_ _Cuban_ immigrants reached south Florida by boat. The U.S.
    government considered this a humanitarian crisis because of the repressive _government in_
    Haita and Cuba. and they were _asylum-seeker_ to the United States.
3. When migrants send money back home to their family, they are called _Remittances_.
    Haitians living in the United States., Canada, and the Caribbean sent over $1 billion in
    remittances in 2007, equivalent to _30_ % of Haiti's gross domestic product.
4. Not all immigrants are undocumented or _illegal_. Of the estimated 31.2 million
    immigrants, _20.4_ are legal.
5. In Canada the vast majority of agricultural workers are from _Mexico_. _(nafta)_

WHAT IS MIGRATION?

from rural to urban.

6. _Movement_ is inherently geographical.
7. _Cyclic_ movement involves shorter periods away from home. _periodic_ involves longer
    periods away from home.
8. _Migration_ movement involves a degree of permanence as the mover may never return
    "home."
9. One's daily routine makes up what geographers call _activity_ _spaces._ and are
    journeys that start and end at our home.
10. _Commuting_ is an example of cyclic movement. In Washington, D.C., workers
    may travel up to _60_ miles a day each way.
11. A type of cyclic movement found in parts of Africa and Asia where movement takes place
    along the same long-familiar routes is known as _Nomadism._
12. _periodic_ movement involves longer periods away from home and activities such as _(migrant labor)_
    transhumance and _Military Service_ service that involves as many as 10 million citizens.
13. _International_ _migration._ occurs across country borders. _(transnational migration)_
14. _Internal_ _migration_ involves moving within a country. Between 1900 and
    1970, African Americans fled from the _South_ to the _North_. Most migration streams
    in the United States have flocked to the _____ and _____ _____.
15. In Peru, most migrants moved to _Lima (the capital)_
    from rural areas.

WHY DO PEOPLE MIGRATE?

16. Migration can be the result of voluntary action, a _conscious_ decision to move from one place to the next. It can also be the result of _involuntary action_, or forced movement.

17. _Voluntary migration_ occurs when a migrant weighs options and choices and involves a migrant making the decision to move.

18. The Irish migration to North America in the mid-1800s is an example of both _forced_ and _voluntary_ migration.   (12 million to 30 million)

19. The _Atlantic slave trade_ is the largest example of forced migration. During the 1930s in Germany, the _Nazis_ were responsible for significant forced migration of the Jews.

20. _Ernst Ravenstein_ proposed the laws of migration. According to the laws of migration, every migration generates a return or _counter migration_. The majority of migrants move a _short_ distance. Urban residents are _less migratory_ than rural peoples. Migrants who move longer distances tend to choose _big-city destination_. _families_ are less likely to make international moves.

21. The _gravity model_ states that the interaction of places is related to the size and _distance between them_.   Population.

22. _Pull factors_ are the circumstances that effectively attract the migrant to certain locales from other places. Push factors – condition and perception that help migrant to leave a place.

23. The idea of _distance decay_ says that as distance increases, interaction decreases.

24. When migrants move in a series of stages—from village to town to city—it is called _step migration_.

25. When hypothetically driving to Florida but finding something else along the way instead, you are captured by an _intervening opportunity_.

26. Gender, ethnicity, race, and _money_ are all factors in the decision to _migrate_.

27. Throughout history oppressive regimes have _engendered_ migration streams. Migrants fled _Vietnam_ after thousands of communists took control of the country. More than 125,000 _Cubans_ were expelled during the communist rule in 1980. (mariel boatlift)

28. Armed conflict drove as many as 3 million people from the _their home (former Yugoslavia)_ to western Europe.

29. A major example of migration induced by environmental conditions was the movement of thousands from _Irish_ to the New World because of the _potato blight_.

30. People who fear that their _culture_ and _tradition_ might not survive will also migrate to safer places. An example of this is when the British partitioned _south Asia_ for Hindus and _pakistan_ for Muslims.

31. Advances in communication technology strengthen the role of _kinship links_ as push or pull factors.

32. When a migrant uses media (phone, e-mail, etc.) to communicate and encourage friends and family to move to where the migrant is located it is known as _chain migration_

_____. A result of this is _immigration wave_ or swells of migration from one origin to the same destination.

WHERE DO PEOPLE MIGRATE?

33. Migration depends on various _push_ and _pull_ factors, ranging from persecution to civil war.

34. _global-scale migration_ rarely occurred before 1500. In the early 1800s, European _explorers_ played a role in mapping the world. _Colonization_ resulted, the physical process whereby the colonizer takes over another place, putting its _own_ _government_ in charge.

35. The major routes of migration before 1500 were as follows: Western Europe to _North America_, Southern Europe to _South/Central America_, Eastern Europe to _Africa/Australia_. South Asia to _Eastern Africa_, East Asia to _America Caribbean_, Africa to _America_ and Britain and Ireland to _Africa/Australia_

36. Islands of development are often _economic development_ because of trade purposes.

37. In the 1800s and early 1900s, millions of _____ labors fled and went to _____ _____ as contract laborers.

38. The center of U.S. population has moved further _west_ since 1790–2000. In 1850, the center was _middle west (Kansas city)_ (Figure 3.16).

39. During the communist period, the Soviet government employed a policy of _Russification_, which sought to _assimilate_ all of the people in the Soviet territory into Russian culture. The main idea behind this was to get Russians to migrate out of _Moscow_ and _St.peterburg_.

40. After _WWI_ many countries in western Europe found themselves in need of _labors_. Many came from outside areas such as _North Africa_. Western European governments called the labor migrants _guest workers_.

41. A _Refugee_ is a person with a well-founded fear of being persecuted for reasons of race, religion, nationality, or membership of a particular social group or political opinion. The right to protection in the first country in which the refugee arrives and possible assistance is known as _asylum_. In the 1990s hostilities broke out between the _Hutu_ and the _Tutsi_ that led to genocide.

42. Today the regions of _North Africa_ and _South west Asia_ generate more than half of the refugees worldwide. The _Iraq (Kuwait)_ invasion of Afghanistan led to many refugees leaving the country. The Taliban coming to power led to a migration of refugees to neighboring _Iran_. During the last decade of the twentieth century and the first years of the twenty-first, several of the world's largest refugee crises occurred in _SubSaharan Africa._.

43. _genocide_ is defined by acts committed with intent to destroy, in whole or in part, a national, ethical, racial, or religious group. The violence in Darfur eventually led to a _____ in 2011 for separation between the north and south. _page 106._

44. The collapse of _yugoskuia_ created the greatest refugee crisis in Europe. In the Western Hemisphere, only _south Asia_ has a serious internally displaced person problem.

HOW DO GOVERNMENTS AFFECT MIGRATION?

page 108

45. Typically, the obstacles placed in the way of potential immigrants are _legal_, not physical.

46. The first immigration law in the United States _____ _____ _____ to prevent _Chinese_ from migrating to California.

47. _quotas_ place limits on immigration, restricting Japanese, and immigration from southern and eastern Europe. Many countries practice _Seletive immigration_, in which individuals with certain backgrounds are barred from entering.

Step 4: Remember to fill out World Region Map Sheets.

Go to the Student Companion Website to print out the sheets: www.wiley.com/college/Fouberg

Step 5: Practice Quiz

Chapter 3: Migration

Multiple Choice Questions

1. What is the name for the seasonal migration of farmers and their cattle up and down the mountain slopes of Switzerland?
    A. internal migration
    B. commuting
    C. activity spaces
    D. transhumance
    E. voluntary migration

2. In mathematical terms, it is the multiplication of the populations of two places divided by the distance between them.
    A. law of migration
    B. intervening opportunity
    C. push-pull equation
    D. transhumance
    E. gravity model

3. What minority group in Southeast Asia accounts for 14% of the population in Thailand, 32% in Malaysia, and 76% in Singapore?
    A. Tamil Indians
    B. Chinese
    C. Sri Lankans
    D. Filipinos
    E. Burmese

4. Which of the following is an example of chain migration?
    A. drought leads to famine in the Punjab, which leads to desperation, which leads to emigration
    B. the Dutch first brought people from Indonesia to the Caribbean, and then from other Dutch colonies around the world
    C. one village after another comes under attack by rebels, forcing the people of those villages to migrate to safer areas
    D. in a rural town in Jalisco, Mexico, one person manages to migrate legally to the United States and settles in Elgin, Illinois. He finds a job and prospers, and writes home of his success. Ten years later there is a community of 350 people from Jalisco living in Elgin.
    E. refers specifically to migrations from Central America, starting in Mexico, then moving through the Central American states of Guatemala, Belize, Honduras, Nicaragua, El Salvador, Costa Rica, and finally Panama

5. Which of the following was NOT given as a reason for the disparity between the UN's calculation of global refugees and the numbers given by other organizations?
    A. the UN inflates the numbers, thus requiring a bigger budget to provide aid to refugees
    B. there are different definitions for what constitutes a refugee
    C. refugees often flee to remote areas where they cannot be counted
    D. governments sometimes manipulate refugee numbers for political reasons
    E. a distinction is made between internal and international refugees

6. Which of the following is a consequence of the large number of men who died in both world wars?
    A. large numbers of North Africans (e.g., Algerians) migrated to German-speaking countries
    B. after the war, women replaced men in factory jobs
    C. Germany, in particular, brought in guest workers, mainly from Turkey
    D. most European countries adopted restrictive immigration policies
    E. the center of European population shifted to the southeast

7.   What is one of the consequences of the fences the United States builds along the border with Mexico, especially those separating cities on both sides of the border?
   A.   since the fences are designed to be attractive and friendly, relations between the countries have improved
   B.   U.S. companies are investing in more maquiladoras
   C.   desperate migrants have started carrying guns and confronting the border patrol
   D.   remittances from the United States to Mexico have been sharply reduced
   E.   it forces illegal immigrants to cross in hostile terrain, such as deserts, leading to more people dying

8.   The practice of barring certain individuals (those with criminal records, poor health, subversive activities) from coming into the country is known as
   A.   selective immigration
   B.   internal migration
   C.   quota system
   D.   forced migration
   E.   chain migration

9.   Which of the following crops is most associated with the forced migration of African slaves?
   A.   plantains
   B.   wheat
   C.   cotton
   D.   rice
   E.   sugar

10. Which of these sets of states had an increase of immigration during both the 1990–2000 and 2000–2004 periods?
   A.   Nebraska—Virginia—New Mexico—California
   B.   Arkansas—Nevada—Georgia—Missouri
   C.   Wisconsin—New York—Wyoming—Pennsylvania
   D.   Illinois—Ohio—Michigan—California
   E.   Minnesota—Mississippi—Indiana—Utah

CHAPTER 4:
LOCAL CULTURE, POPULAR CULTURE, AND CULTURAL LANDSCAPES

The Five Steps to Chapter Success

Step 1: Read the Chapter Summary below, preview the Key Questions, the Chapter Outline, and the Geographic Concepts of the chapter.

Step 2: Complete the Pre-Reading Activity (PRA) for this chapter.

Step 3: Read the chapter and complete the guided worksheet.

Step 4: As you read the chapter, complete World Region Map Sheets for every world map.
Go to the Student Companion Website to print out the WRMS.

Step 5: Take an AP-style Practice Quiz.

STEP 1: Chapter Summary, Key Questions, Chapter Outline, and Geographic Concepts

Chapter Summary

Advances in transportation and communications technology help popular culture diffuse at record speeds around the world today. Popular culture changes quickly, offering new music, foods, fashions, and sports. Popular culture envelopes and infiltrates local cultures, presenting constant challenges to members of local cultures. Some members of local cultures have accepted popular culture, others have rejected it, and still others have forged a balance between the two.

Customs from local cultures are often commodified, propelling them into popular culture. The search for an "authentic" local culture custom generally ends up promoting a stereotyped local culture or glorifying a single aspect of that local culture. Local culture, like popular culture, is dynamic, and the pursuit of authenticity disregards the complexity and fluidity of cultures.

Key Questions

Field Note: Preserving Culture	112–113
1. What are local and popular cultures?	113–116
2. How are local cultures sustained?	116–126
3. How is popular culture diffused?	126–136

Chapter 4 Outline

A.   What Are Local and Popular Cultures?

B.   How Are Local Cultures Sustained?

    1.   Rural Local Cultures

        a.   The Makah American Indians

        b.   Little Sweden, U.S.A.

    2.   Urban Local Cultures

    3.   Local Cultures and Cultural Appropriation

    4.   Authenticity of Places

        a.   Guinness and the Irish Pub Company

C.   How Is Popular Culture Diffused?

    1.   Hearths of Popular Culture

        a.   Establishing a Hearth

        b.   Manufacturing a Hearth

    2.   Replacing Old Hearths with New: Beating Out the Big Three in Popular Sports

    3.   Stemming the Tide of Popular Culture—Losing the Local?

D.   How Can Local and Popular Cultures Be Seen in the Cultural Landscape?

    1.   Cultural Landscapes of Local Cultures

Geographic Concepts		
Culture	Assimilation	Time–Space Compression
Folk Culture	Custom	Reterritorialization
Popular Culture	Cultural Appropriation	Cultural Landscape
Local Culture	Neolocalism	Placelessness
Material Culture	Ethnic Neighborhood	Global-Local Continuum
Nonmaterial Culture	Commodification	Glocalization
Hierarchical Diffusion	Authenticity	Folk-Housing Regions
Hearth	Distance Decay	Diffusion Routes

Step 2: Pre-Reading Activity (PRA)

Name: _____ **Period** _____   **Date** _____

Chapter Title _____

Chapter # _____   **Pgs.** _____ to _____

1. Write down each of the Key Questions and the number of pages for each (go back to Step 1 of your textbook for answers).

Key Question	# of Pages

2. After looking over the Key Questions and looking through the outline, write a few sentences about what you expect to learn in general in this chapter.

3. Preview the entire chapter and look at all the maps, tables, charts and pictures. Read the captions. Briefly describe IN YOUR OWN WORDS five maps or charts.

pg. _____ _____

pg. _____ _____

pg. _____ _____

pg. _____ _____

pg. _____ _____

4. How many world maps are there in this chapter? _____ (Go to the Student Companion Website and print out the World Map Region Worksheets needed for this chapter.)

5.   Read the Field Note introduction of the chapter and list five specific facts you learned.

_____

_____

_____

_____

_____

_____

_____

_____

_____

_____

6.   Go to Step 1 and look at the Geographic Concepts. Create a list of terms you think you know and terms you need to know.

I THINK I KNOW	I NEED TO LEARN

Step 3: Chapter 4 Guided Worksheet (Created by Parisa Watson)

Name: _____ **Period** _____ **Date** _____

Directions: As you read the chapter, fill in the blanks on the guided worksheet.

FIELD NOTE—PRESERVING CULTURE

1. The Tata family are members of the ___parsi___ ethnic group and religion. They are followers of the ___Zoroastrian___ religion and came to India from ___persia___ between the eighth and tenth centuries.

2. Despite the fact that the Parsi make up only 0.00046% of the population, they control a ___large___ share of the Indian economy.

3. A local culture such as the Parsi is maintained through the preservation of ___cultural___ ___trait___ and practices. The Parsi religion only recognizes members of children born to ___2___ Parsi parents.

4. The Parsi have high literacy rates and many women choose not to ___marry___ or have ___children___ late, reducing the fertility rate.

WHAT ARE LOCAL AND POPULAR CULTURES?

5. A ___Culture___ is a group of belief systems, norms and values practiced by a people. Although the definition is simple, the concept of culture is actually quite _____.

6. The idea is that ___folk___ ___culture___ is small, incorporates a homogeneous population, is typically rural, and is cohesive in cultural traits.

7. ___popular___ ___culture___ is usually large, incorporates heterogeneous populations, is typically urban, and experiences quick changes.

8. ___folk___ ___culture___ is a limiting concept because it requires the creation of a list of characteristics and search for cultures that meet that list. The chapter chooses the concept of ___local___ ___culture___ over folk culture. It consists of a group of ___people___ in a particular place who see themselves as a community and share experiences and customs.

9. ___material___ ___culture___ includes things a group of people construct, such as art, houses, clothing, sports, dance and foods.

10. ___nonmaterial___ ___culture___ includes the beliefs, practices, aesthetics, and values of a group of people. What members of a local culture produce in their material culture reflects the ___belief___ and ___values___ of their nonmaterial culture.

11. Fashion is an example of ___hierarchial___ diffusion. The order of the fashion world begins with the runways of major fashion cities, including London, ___milan___, Paris and New York. These cities act as ___hearths___, or points of origin.

HOW ARE LOCAL CULTURES SUSTAINED?

12. In the 1800s into the 1900s, the U.S. government had a policy of _assimilation_. This attempted to make American Indians into "_American_."

13. Local cultures are sustained through _custom_, a practice that a group of people routinely follow. To sustain a local culture, people must maintain their _customs_.

14. A local culture can also work to avoid _cultural appropriation_, the process by which other cultures adopt customs and knowledge and use them for their own benefit.

15. The Hutterites differ from the Amish in that they _readily accept technologies_. They speak _archaic German_. The Hutterites live in the following states and Canadian provinces: _WA, Oregon, Montana, North Dakota/South, Minesota_

16. The Makah American Indians wanted to hunt _whales_. They wanted to hunt them with _traditional harpoon (canoe or)_ but were instead forced to use _.50 Calibear rifle_.

17. "Little Sweden" in Lindsborg, Kansas, is an example of _neolocalism_, or seeking out the regional culture reinvigorating it in response to the uncertainty in the modern world.

18. Some local cultures are able to practice their customs in large cities by constructing _ethnic neighborhoods_. Runners of the New York City Marathon can see them in Brooklyn, as they pass through Mexican neighborhoods as well as _Hasidic Jewish_ neighborhoods.

19. _Commodification_ involves taking an object that was not previously sold and making it something that is sold on the world market.

20. When this occurs, it can lead to the development of an image of _authenticity_, which amounts to cultural stereotyping. The city of _Branson_, Missouri, capitalizes on a local culture in the Ozarks.

21. The Irish Beer Pub is part of the _Guinness Brewing_ brand of Dublin, Ireland. The company has built over 400 pubs in _40_ countries around the world.

HOW IS POPULAR CULTURE DIFFUSED?

22. During the twentieth century, the pace of diffusion has _shrank_ to months, weeks, days and in some cases even _hours_. At the same time, the _spatial_ extent of diffusion has _expanded_.

23. Transportation and communication have altered _distance decay_. Time–space compression explains how quickly innovations diffuse and refers to how interlinked two places are through _transportation_ and _communication technology_.

24. The Dave Matthews Band is an example of _hierarchal_ diffusion as they started in _hierarchal or college_.

25. _reterritorialization_ happens when people start to produce an aspect of popular culture for themselves and make it their own. This is visible through _gangsta rap_ in countries such as France.

Pg 118

26. While sports such as _____, _____ and _____ are historically popular in the United States, _____ _____ such as skating, snowboarding, and ultimate fighting are gaining appeal.

27. Popular media from the _____ and _____ diffuse quickly. Most video games are created in _____.

HOW CAN LOCAL AND POPULAR CULTURES BE SEEN IN THE CULTURAL LANDSCAPE?

28. __placelessness__ describes the loss of uniqueness of place in the cultural landscape as places look more alike. Places can begin to blend together and have similar _three dimesions_ styles, _business_ can leave a distinctive landscape stamp on faraway places, and idealized _landscape Image_ are often borrowed. _skyscrapers_ in places such as Chicago, Singapore, and Johannesburg are examples of this concept.

29. Reading signs is an easy way to see cultural landscape convergence. Seeing signs for businesses in Rome such as _Blockbuster / McDonald_ are an example. The strip in _Los vegas_ has various structures to evoke different parts of the planet.

30. The idea that what happens at one scale is not independent of what happens at other scales is known as the _global-local continuum_. When people at a local scale alter regional, national, or global processes, it is called _globalization_.

31. Founders and early followers of the Church of Jesus Christ of _latter-day_ Saints created the _mormon_ landscape of the American West. They migrated to the West because of _persecution_ to freely practice their _religion_. They eventually migrated to present-day _Salt-lake city utah_.

Step 4: Remember to fill out World Region Map Sheets.

Go to the Student Companion Website to print out the sheets: www.wiley.com/college/ Fouberg

Step 5: Practice Quiz

Chapter 4: Local Culture, Popular Culture, and Cultural Landscapes

Multiple Choice Questions

1. How do the Hutterites differ from the Amish?
    A. Hutterites wear clothing that is less traditional than the Amish
    B. the Amish wear clothing that is less traditional than the Hutterites
    C. Hutterite children will attend regular public schools
    D. Hutterites readily accept technologies that help their agricultural work
    E. the Amish readily accept technologies that help their agricultural work

2. Which of the following statements about St. Patrick's Day is true?
    A. it transcends ethnicity to be celebrated as part of popular culture
    B. the traditional red colors of St. Patrick's Day represents the blood of the Irish Catholic martyrs
    C. Protestant Christians generally eschew St. Patrick's Day festivities
    D. the parade is a form of urban local culture
    E. it is customary for women in the parade to wear a corset bodice dress

3. What are the two goals of local cultures?
    A. to commodify their material and nonmaterial culture
    B. to escape persecution and find a place to practice their religion
    C. to preserve tradition and assimilate with local residents
    D. to appropriate the customs of other cultures and make them authentically their own
    E. to keep other cultures out and keep their own culture in

4. What is the greatest challenge to urban local cultures?
    A. migration of "others" into their neighborhoods
    B. deterioration of housing stock
    C. discrimination by the mainstream culture
    D. dissemination of popular culture through media
    E. a younger generation not interested in the old ways

5. The rapid diffusion of innovations through modern technology that quickly links distant locations is known as
    A. distance decay
    B. authenticity transmission
    C. reterritorialization
    D. time–space compression
    E. placelessness

6. The common American house type known as the "ranch" style
    A. is a variation of the New England style
    B. was designed to efficiently retain heat
    C. originated in the West and diffused eastward
    D. usually has two stories
    E. resembles the saltboxes of the nineteenth century

7.   What was the policy by which the U.S. government tried to make Native Americans more like Americans of European (white) descent?
     A.   cultural appropriation
     B.   ethnic reformation
     C.   neolocalism
     D.   assimilation
     E.   commodification

8.   Distance decay ensures that
     A.   the quality of an innovation decreases with distance from its hearth
     B.   diseases and decay will spread faster in the 21st century
     C.   better connected cities, regardless of distance, will receive innovations quicker than nearby but less connected locations
     D.   the authenticity of a cultural trait decreases as it diffuses globally
     E.   a cultural innovation, once it diffuses widely, cannot be traced back to its original hearth

9.   Kids in Katmandu, Nepal, wear the styles and listen to the music of Hip Hop culture, but with Nepalese accents. This type of diffusion is called
     A.   hearth diffusion
     B.   relocation
     C.   phishing
     D.   contagious diffusion
     E.   reterritorialization

10. Which of the following is an example of cultural appropriation?
     A.   extreme sports becoming mainstream sports
     B.   Japan's adoption of Western technology in the late 1800s, but not the West's cultural values
     C.   an American rural community descended from Germans deciding to have an annual German festival
     D.   celebrities adopting some aspect of a local culture, resulting in that local culture becoming more accessible to popular culture trends
     E.   the homogenization of the world's cultural landscape (McDonaldization)

CHAPTER 5:
IDENTITY: RACE, ETHNICITY, GENDER, AND SEXUALITY

The Five Steps to Chapter Success Checklist

> Step 1: Read the Chapter Summary below, preview the Key Questions, the Chapter Outline, and
> the terms of the chapter.
> Step 2: Complete the Pre-Reading Activity (PRA) for this chapter.
> Step 3: Read the chapter and complete the guided worksheet.
> Step 4: As you read the chapter, complete World Region Map Sheets for every world map.
> Go to the Student Companion Website to print out the WRMS.
> Step 5: Take an AP-style Practice Quiz.

STEP 1: Chapter Summary, Key Questions, Chapter Outline, and Geographic Concepts

Chapter Summary

Identity is a powerful concept. The way we make sense of ourselves is a personal journey that is mediated and influenced by the political, social, and cultural contexts in which we live and work. Group identities such as gender, ethnicity, race, and sexuality are constructed, both by self-realization and by identifying against and across scales. When learning about new places and different people, humans are often tempted to put places and people into boxes, into myths or stereotypes that make them easily digestible.

The geographer, especially one who spends time in the field, recognizes that how people shape and create places varies across time and space and that time, space, and place shape people, both individually and in groups. James Curtis ably described the work of a geographer who studies places: "But like the popular images and stereotypical portrayals of all places—whether positive or negative, historical or contemporary—these mask a reality on the ground that is decidedly more complex and dynamic, from both the economic and social perspectives." What Curtis says about places is true about people as well. What we may *think* to be positive identities, such as the myths of "Orientalism" or of the "model minority," and what we know are negative social ills, such as racism and dowry deaths, are all decidedly more complex and dynamic than they first seem.

Key Questions

Field Note: Building Walls	144–146
1. What is identity, and how are identities constructed?	146–154
2. How do places affect identity, and how can we see identities in places?	155–158
3. How does geography reflect and shape power relationships among groups of people?	159–170

Chapter 5 Outline

A. What Is Identity, and How Are Identities Constructed?

    1. Race

    2. Race and Ethnicity in the United States

    3. Residential Segregation

    4. Identities Across Scales

    5. The Scale of New York City

B. How Do Places Affect Identity, and How Can We See Identities in Places?

    1. Ethnicity and Place

        a. Chinatwom in Mexicali

    2. Identity and Space

        a. Sexuality and Space

C. How Does Geography Reflect and Shape Power Relationships Among Groups?

    1. Just Who Counts?

    2. Vulnerable Populations

    3. Women in Subsaharan Africa

    4. Dowry Deaths in India

    5. Shifting Power Relations among Ethnic Groups

        a. Power Relations in Los Angeles

Geographic Concepts		
Gender	Succession	Queer Theory
Identity	Sense of Place	Dowry Deaths
Identifying Against	Ethnicity	Barrioization
Race	Space	Place
Racism	Place	Gendered
Residential Segregation	Gendered	Queer Theory

Step 2: Pre-Reading Activity (PRA)

Name: _____ **Period** _____ **Date** _____

Chapter Title: _____

Chapter # _____   **Pgs.** _____ to _____

1. Write down each of the Key Questions and the number of pages for each (go back to Step 1 of your textbook for answers).

Key Question	# of Pages

2. After looking over the Key Questions, looking through the outline, and reading the chapter summary, write a few sentences about what you expect to learn in general in this chapter.

3. Preview the entire chapter and look at all the maps, tables, charts, and pictures. Read the captions. Briefly describe IN YOUR OWN WORDS five maps or charts.

    pg. _____ _____

    pg. _____ _____

    pg. _____ _____

    pg. _____ _____

    pg. _____ _____

4. How many world maps are there in this chapter? _____ (Go to the Student Companion Website and print out the World Map Region Worksheets needed for this chapter.)

5. Read the Field Note introduction of the chapter and list five specific facts you learned.

    _____

    _____

    _____

    _____

    _____

    _____

    _____

    _____

    _____

    _____

6.   Go to Step 1 and look at the Geographic Concepts. Create a list of terms you think you know and terms you need to know.

I THINK I KNOW	I NEED TO LEARN

Step 3: Chapter 5 Guided Worksheet (Created by Parisa Watson)

Name: _____ **Period** _____ **Date** _____

Directions: As you read the chapter, fill in the blanks on the guided worksheet.

FIELD NOTE—BUILDING WALLS

1.   The women in Bali work _ten hours_ a day turning, stacking, and restacking bricks for _45 cent_ an hour. More than a century ago, bricks were made this way in the _US_.

2.   In Bali, most brick-makers are _boy_ and _women_. In the United States, the majority are _men/robot_ and aided by machines.

3.   Gender is defined as a culture's _assumption_ about the differences between _men_ and _woman_.

4.   Societies create boxes in which we put people and expect them to _live_. These create a _stereotypes_ and assumptions we make about what is expected about women, men, and members of certain races or _ethnic_ groups, and people with various sexual preferences.

5.   In creating these boxes, society can assign an entire _profession_ or tasks to members of certain categories.

WHAT IS IDENTITY, AND HOW ARE IDENTITIES CONSTRUCTED?

6. _Identity_ is how we make sense of ourselves. It is constructed through our own _identities_, emotions, connections and rejections.

7. One of the most powerful ways to construct an identity is by _identifying against_ other people. This involves defining the "_Other_," and then we define _ourselves._ in opposing terms.

8. _Race_ is a combination of physical attributes such as skin color.

9. Socioeconomic differences can fuel a sense of superiority attached to race known as _racism_.

10. Differences in skin color, eye color, and hair color likely result from a long history of _adaptation_ to different environments.

11. People have different skin colors because of different amounts of _Melanin_. Most people are deficient in _____ because they don't get enough sunlight. Unlike ethnicity, race is often an identity that is _more often assigned_.

Pg 147

12. Hispanic, then, is not a _race_ but is better defined as an _ethnicity_.

13. _residential segregation_ is when people of different groups live separate from one another.

14. The 2002 Census Bureau report found that overall residential segregation by race/ethnicity is on the _decline_.

15. _Succession_ is the most racially segregated city in the United States. Most African Americans in that city are concentrated in the _upper manhattan_. _wa height_

16. The way we make sense of ourselves in an increasingly _____ world is complex. We have different identities at different _____.

HOW DO PLACES AFFECT IDENTITY, AND HOW CAN WE SEE IDENTITIES IN PLACES?

17. Peoples' sense of place _____ over time because places are constantly evolving.

18. The idea of _____ as an identity stems from the notion that people are closely bounded, even related, in a certain place over time.

19. Ethos means "_____" or "_____" and ethnic identity is more cultural.

20. The border region between the United States and _____ is often seen as a meeting point between Mexico and Anglo Americans. The ethnic region in the border region is more _____ than Mexican and Anglo.

21. The town of _____ is the capital of the State of Baja California.

22. The _____ in Mexicali were prominent players in the social and economic life of the city during the twentieth century. The town is experiencing a transformation, as the _____ residents have dispersed to the edges of the city and beyond. Relatively _____ live in the city's Chinatown.

23. Space is defined as _____ relations stretched out, and _____ as particular articulations of those social relations as they have come together.
24. Places designed for women or for men are known as _____.
25. Many geographers who study sexuality are employing _____ _____ in their studies.

HOW DOES GEOGRAPHY REFLECT AND SHAPE POWER RELATIONSHIPS AMONG GROUPS OF PEOPLE?

26. _____ _____ are assumptions and structures about who is in control and who has power over others.
27. Policies created by governments can limit access of certain _____. _____ _____ laws in the United States once separated "black" spaces from "white" spaces.
28. Prior to the Fourteenth Amendment, a black person counted as _____ of a white person. Until 1924, the U.S. government did not recognize the right of all _____ _____ to vote, even though the Fifteenth Amendment recognized the right to vote regardless of race in 1870.
29. Not until 1920 did enough states ratify the _____ Amendment, which recognized the right of all Americans to vote regardless of _____.
30. Throughout the world, the work of _____ is often undervalued and uncounted. GNI does not count the unpaid labor of _____ in the household, nor the work done by _____ _____ in LDCs.
31. *The World's Women 2010* reported _____ variation in agricultural employment for women. In Africa, the ranges were between _____ and _____, while in eastern Asia, the agricultural percentage is _____.
32. _____ _____ occur in India and involve a bride's family not paying the groom's family, leading to the death of the bride. The practice is not declining as in 2009, the total jumped to _____.
33. The area of southeastern Los Angeles County is today home to one of the largest concentrations of _____ in Southern California.
34. _____ is Spanish for neighborhood. _____ refers to the jump in Hispanic population in a neighborhood.

Step 4: Remember to fill out World Region Map Sheets.

Go to the Student Companion Website to print out the sheets: www.wiley.com/college/Fouberg

Step 5: Practice Quiz

Chapter 5: Identity: Race, Ethnicity, Gender, and Sexuality

Multiple Choice Questions

1. How does "ethnicity" differ from "race?"
    A. there is no difference in common usage
    B. ethnicity implies a religious affiliation; race does not
    C. race is a physiological concept; ethnicity is not linked to genetics
    D. race is something to which we choose to belong; ethnicity is assigned
    E. ethnicity is something to which we choose to belong; race is assigned

2. What U.S. city has the greatest number and diversity of immigrants?
    A. Chicago
    B. Los Angeles
    C. Miami
    D. New York
    E. Seattle

3. State of mind derived through the infusion of a place with meaning and emotion is called
    A. sense of place
    B. ethnicity
    C. ethnic space
    D. queer theory
    E. immigrants

4. Who produces about 70% of the food in rural Subsaharan Africa?
    A. men
    B. women
    C. children
    D. agribusiness companies
    E. immigrants

5. Barrioization refers to
    A. the increasing political clout of Mexican immigrants in big-city politics
    B. the replacement of Anglo-American street names with Spanish street names
    C. neighborhoods, especially in Los Angeles, where the Hispanic population rapidly displaces the original residents
    D. the gerrymandering of voting districts in predominantly Hispanic regions
    E. states where Hispanics will represent a majority population in the next 20 years

6. The most residentially segregated large metropolitan area for African Americans is
    A. Detroit, MI
    B. Orange County, CA
    C. San Francisco, CA
    D. Milwaukee, WI
    E. New York, NY

7. In New York, Puerto Ricans took over Jewish neighborhoods in a process geographers call
    A. residential segregation
    B. ethnic succession
    C. residential invasion
    D. cultural transition
    E. invasion and succession

8. What would happen to the world's gross national income if the work women do at home was calculated at market value?
    A. there is no way to accurately estimate the value of such work
    B. global GNI would remain the same
    C. global GNI would actually decline
    D. global GNI would grow by 10%
    E. global GNI would grow by about one-third

9. Which of the following best describes the relations between Indians and Pakistanis in Fairfax County, Virginia?
    A. they maintain separate food and entertainment businesses
    B. they are spatially segregated in different neighborhoods
    C. they attend the same Hindu temples
    D. they coexist without animosity
    E. tensions occasionally require police intervention

10. What is a term used in the discussion of sexual behavior, gender, and society, primarily within the fields of queer theory and gender theory? It is used to describe (and frequently to criticize) the manner in which many social institutions and social policies are seen to reinforce certain beliefs.
    A. transgender
    B. sexual identity
    C. gendered roles
    D. identity
    E. heteronormative

CHAPTER 6:
LANGUAGE

The Five Steps to Chapter Success Checklist

Step 1: Read the Chapter Summary below, preview the Key Questions, the Chapter Outline, and
the terms of the chapter.

Step 2: Complete the Pre-Reading Activity (PRA) for this chapter.

Step 3: Read the chapter and complete the guided worksheet.

Step 4: As you read the chapter, complete World Region Map sheets for every world map.
Go to the Student Companion Website to print out the WMRS.

Step 5: Take an AP-style Practice Quiz.

STEP 1: Chapter Summary, Key Questions, Chapter Outline and Geographic Concepts

Chapter Summary

The global mosaic of languages reflects centuries of divergence, convergence, extinction, and diffusion. Linguists and linguistic geographers have the interesting work of uncovering, through deep reconstruction, the hearths of the world's language families. Some languages, such as Basque, defy explanation. Other languages are the foci of countless studies, many of which come to differing conclusions about their ancient origins.

As certain languages, such as English and Chinese, gain speakers and become global languages, other languages become extinct. Some languages come to serve as the lingua franca of a region or place. Governments choose official languages, and through public schools, educators entrench an official language in a place. Some countries, faced with the global diffusion of the English language, defend and promote their national language. Whether requiring signs to be written a certain way or requiring a television station to broadcast some proportion of programming in the national language, governments can preserve language, choose a certain dialect as the standard, or repel the diffusion of other languages.

Regardless of the place, the people, or the language used, language continues to define, shape, and maintain culture. How a person thinks about the world is reflected in the words used to describe and define it.

Key Questions

Field Note: What Should I Say?	172–176
What are languages, and what role do languages play in cultures?)	176–182
Why are languages distributed the way they are?	182–191
How do languages diffuse?	192–196
What role does language play in making places?	197–200

Chapter 6 Outline

A. What Are Languages, and What Role Do Languages Play in Cultures?
1. Languages and Culture
2. What Is a Language?
3. Standardized Language
4. Dialects

B. Why Are Languages Distributed the Way They Are?
1. Definition and Debate
2. Language Formation
   a. Reconstructing the Vocabulary of Proto Indo-European and Its Ancient Ancestor
   b. Locating the Hearth of Proto-Indo-European
   c. Tracing the Routes of Diffusion of Proto-Indo-European
3. The Languages of Europe
   a. The Subfamilies
   b. Language and Politics
4. Languages of Subsaharan Africa

C. How Do Languages Diffuse?
1. Lingua Franca
2. Multilingualism
3. Official Languages
4. Global Language

D. What Role Does Language Play in Making Places?
1. The Ten Toponyms
2. Toponyms and Globalization
3. Changing Toponyms
   a. Postcolonial Toponyms
   b. Postrevolution Toponyms
   c. Memorial Toponyms
   d. Commodification of Toponyms

Geographic Concepts		
Language	Backward Reconstruction	Slavic Languages
Culture	Extinct Language	Lingua Franca
Mutual Intelligibility	Deep Reconstruction	Pidgin Language
Standard Language	Nostratic	Creole Language
Dialects	Language Divergence	Monolingual States
Dialect Chains	Language Convergence	Multilingual States
Isogloss	Renfrew Hypothesis	Official Language
Language Families	Conquest Theory	Global Language
Subfamilies	Dispersal Hypothesis	Place
Sound Shift	Romance Languages	Toponym
Proto-Indo-European	Germanic Languages	

Step 2: Pre-Reading Activity (PRA)

Name: _____ **Period** _____ **Date** _____

Chapter Title: _____

Chapter # _____   **Pgs.** _____ **to** _____

1. Write down each of the Key Questions and the number of pages for each (go back to Step 1 of your textbook for answers).

Key Question	# of Pages

2. After looking over the Key Questions, looking through the outline, and reading the chapter summary, write a few sentences about what you expect to learn in general in this chapter.

3.   Preview the entire chapter and look at all the maps, tables, charts, and pictures. Read the captions. Briefly describe IN YOUR OWN WORDS five maps or charts.

pg. _____ _____

pg. _____ _____

pg. _____ _____

pg. _____ _____

pg. _____ _____

4.   How many world maps are there in this chapter? _____ (Go to the Student Companion Website and print out the World Map Region Worksheets needed for this chapter.)

5.   Read the Field Note introduction of the chapter and list five specific facts you learned.

_____

_____

_____

_____

_____

_____

_____

_____

_____

_____

6.   Go to Step 1 and look at the Geographic Concepts. Create a list of terms you think you know and terms you need to know.

I THINK I KNOW	I NEED TO LEARN

Step 3: Chapter 6 Guided Worksheet (Created by Parisa Watson)

Name: _____ **Period** _____ **Date** _____

Directions: As you read the chapter, fill in the blanks on the guided worksheet.

FIELD NOTE—WHAT SHOULD I SAY?

1. In stores throughout _____,_____ you can see the capital city's _____ all around you.
2. The map (Figure 6.3) shows _____ spoken in the northern region of Flanders and _____ spoken in the southern region of Wallonia.
3. Brussels is also the capital of the _____.

WHAT ARE LANGUAGES, AND WHAT ROLE DO LANGUAGES PLAY IN CULTURES?

4. With the support of many French people, the French government passed a _____ in 1975 banning the use of _____ words in advertisements, televisions, radio broadcasts, and official documents. They have also passed laws to stop the use of foreign words in France, with a hefty _____ imposed for violators.
5. Language is a set of _____ and _____ used for communication.
6. The language with the most number of speakers is Mandarin _____. Most Internet content is in _____ (Figure 6.4).
7. A few U.S. states are bilingual, such as _____.
8. The country of Canada is officially _____, speaking English and _____. Most of the country's French speakers live in the province of _____. The majority of people there speak _____ at home.
9. _____ _____ means when two people can understand each other when speaking.
10. Technologically advanced societies are likely to have a _____ _____, one that is published, widely distributed, and purposefully taught.
11. Variants of a standard language are known as _____.
12. An _____ is a geographic boundary within which a particular linguistic feature occurs, such as that among soft-drink names. In Illinois, the majority would ask for a _____, while in Wisconsin they would ask for a _____ (Figure 6.7).

WHY ARE LANGUAGES DISTRIBUTED THE WAY THEY ARE?

13. _____ _____ have a shared but fairly distant origin while _____ _____ have a more definite and recent origin.
14. There are around _____ language families according to Figure 6.8. The _____ _____ family has the widest distribution and claims the largest number of speakers. _____ is the most widely spoken Indo-European language. Hundreds of millions of people speak versions of _____ as a second or third language.

15. A sound shift is a slight change in a _____ within a language family. For example, the Latin word for milk, _____, becomes _____ in Italian, _____ in Spanish, and _____ in French.
16. _____ is the ancestor of the Indo-European language.
17. _____ _____ is used to track sound shifts back in time toward the original language.
18. _____ is the ancestor of the Proto-Indo-European language.
19. _____ _____ occurs when new languages form because of a lack of interaction among speakers. _____ _____ are when consistent interaction evolves into the collapsing of languages.
20. Linguists theorize that the hearth of the Proto-Indo-European language was somewhere in the vicinity of the _____ ____ or east-central Europe.
21. The conquest theory holds that speakers of the Indo-European language spread from _____ to _____ on horseback, overpowering earlier inhabitants and diffusing.
22. Despite the genetic gradient identified in Europe, some linguistic geographers continue to favor the _____ _____, which holds that the Indo-European languages that arose from Proto-Indo-European were first carried eastward into _____ Asia, next around the _____ Sea, and then across the Russian-Ukrainian plains and on into the _____.
23. _____ people brought Indo-European tongues into Europe. They fell victim to _____ migrations and empire building.
24. Spanish, French, and Italian are _____ languages.
25. English, German, Danish, Norwegian, and Swedish are _____ languages.
26. Russian, Polish, and Ukraine are _____ languages.
27. In Subsaharan Africa, the _____ family dominates.
28. _____ is the official language of Nigeria.

HOW DO LANGUAGES DIFFUSE?

29. In the late Middle Ages, the invention of the _____ _____ and the rise of nation-states helped spread literacy and stabilize languages.
30. A _____ _____ is a language used among speakers of different languages for the purpose of trade and commerce. It can be a _____ language or a mixture of ____ or more.
31. When people speaking two or more languages are in contact and they combine parts of their languages in a simplified structure and vocabulary, we call it a _____ language.
32. _____ became a lingua franca during the expansion of _____, as did English during the colonial era. _____ is the lingua franca of East Africa.
33. A _____ _____ is a pidgin language that has developed a more complex structure and vocabulary and has become the native language of a group of people.

34. _____ countries are those countries where everyone virtually speaks the same language. Countries in which more than one language is in use are called _____ _____.

35. Countries with linguistic fragmentation often adopt an _____ _____.

36. The three **main** language families of India: _____, _____, _____.

WHAT ROLE DOES LANGUAGE PLAY IN MAKING PLACES?

37. Each _____ has a unique location and constitutes a reflection of human activities, ideas, and tangible, durable creations.

38. _____ refer to place names.

39. Most Brazilian toponyms are _____, reflecting colonization.

40. _____ prompts name changes. In 1997, the revolutionary leader Laurent Kabila ousted Mobutu and established his regime in the capital, _____. He also renamed the country _____.

41. Most cities with the street Martin Luther King are located in the _____.

42. The practice of _____ toponyms is growing, especially in areas largely within the fold of popular culture. Stadiums such as _____ are examples of this phenomenon.

Step 4: Remember to fill out World Region Map Sheets.

Go to the Student Companion Website to print out the sheets: www.wiley.com/college/Fouberg

Step 5: Practice Quiz

Chapter 6: Language

Multiple Choice Questions

1. The predominant languages spoken on Madagascar are not of an African language family but belong to a(n)
    A. Indo-European family
    B. Sino-Tibetan family
    C. Dravidian family
    D. Austronesian family
    E. Altaic family

2. Two Russian scholars have established the core of what they believe is the pre-Proto-Indo-European language named
   A. Nostratic
   B. Anatolian
   C. Etruscan
   D. Austronesian
   E. Aryano-Armenic

3. A geographic boundary within which a particular linguistic feature occurs is called a/an
   A. isotherm
   B. sound shift
   C. international border
   D. cultural boundary
   E. isogloss

4. Hawaii and Louisiana are states that have
   A. no linguistic variation
   B. official "English only" policies
   C. official bilingual policies
   D. no official language policies
   E. Creole populations

5. Which of the following European countries has a rather sharp division between Flemish speakers in the north and Walloon speakers in the south?
   A. The Netherlands
   B. Belgium
   C. Denmark
   D. Andorra
   E. Switzerland

6. The Indo-European language family prevails on the map of Europe. Which country listed below has a language that is not in the Indo-European family?
   A. France
   B. Italy
   C. Iceland
   D. Luxembourg
   E. Hungary

7. Bantu migrations marginalized this once widespread African language family that now is found only in dry regions of southwestern Africa.
    A. Niger-Congo family
    B. Khoisan family
    C. Afro-Asiatic family
    D. Sudanic subfamily
    E. Gaelic subfamily

8. In an attempt to deal with linguistic as well as cultural diversity, many former African colonies have taken as their official language
    A. the most widely spoken indigenous language
    B. an Austronesian and therefore neutral language
    C. the language of the former colonial power
    D. an invented language with no historical connections
    E. Swahili, the lingua franca of all of Africa

9. When African colonies became independent countries, one of the first acts of many of the new governments was to
    A. conduct a census
    B. build a new capital city
    C. change the names of places that had been named after colonial figures
    D. build new road systems
    E. seek international aid

10. In technically advanced societies there is likely to be
    A. a standard language
    B. many basic languages
    C. limited expansion of language
    D. standard pronunciation
    E. a lot of technical terms

11. According to the text, dialects are usually marked by differences in all of the following EXCEPT
    A. accents
    B. pronunciation
    C. vocabulary
    D. syntax
    E. diction

12. Convergence processes yielding a synthesis of several languages produce a pidgin language. When this language becomes the first language of a population it is referred to as a

    A. dialect
    B. Creole language
    C. language subfamily
    D. lingua franca
    E. corrupted language

CHAPTER 7:
RELIGION

The Five Steps to Chapter Success Checklist

Step 1: Read the Chapter Summary below, preview the Key Questions, the Chapter Outline, and the terms of the chapter.

Step 2: Complete the Pre-Reading Activity (PRA) for this chapter.

Step 3: Read the chapter and complete the guided worksheet.

Step 4: As you read the chapter, complete World Region Map Sheets for every world map.
    Go to the Student Companion Website to print out the WRMS.

Step 5: Take an AP-style Practice Quiz.

STEP 1: Chapter Summary, Key Questions, Chapter Outline, and Geographic Concepts

Chapter Summary

Religion is a major force in shaping and changing culture. The major world religions today all stem from an area of Eurasia stretching from the eastern Mediterranean to China. Major world religions are distributed regionally, with Hinduism in India; Buddhism, Taoism, Shintoism, and Chinese philosophies in East and Southeast Asia; Islam reaching across North Africa, through the Middle East and into Southeast Asia; Shamanist religions mainly in Subsaharan Africa; and Christianity in Europe, Western Asia, the Americas, Australia, and New Zealand. Judaism, another major world religion, is not as concentrated. Today, Judaism has a base in Israel and has adherents scattered throughout Europe and the Americas.

As the September 11, 2001, attacks on New York City and Washington, D.C., made clear, religious beliefs can drive people to extremist behaviors. On a day-to-day basis, however, religion more typically drives cultures—shaping how people behave, how people perceive the behaviors of others, and how people across place, scale, and time interact with each other.

Key Questions

Field Note: Dying and Resurrecting	203–205
What is religion, and what role does it play in culture?	205–207
Where did the major religions of the world originate, and how do religions diffuse?	208–224
How is religion seen in the cultural landscape?	224–234
What role does religion play in political conflicts?	235–246

Chapter 7 Outline

A.   What Is Religion, and What Role Does It Play in Culture?

B.   Where Did the World's Major Religions Originate, and How Do Religions Diffuse?

    1.   The World Map of Religions Today

    2.   From the Hearth of South Asia

       a.   Hinduism

       b.   The Diffusion of Hinduism

       c.   Buddhism

       d.   Shintoism

    3.   From the Hearth of the Huang He River Valley

       a.   Confucianism

       b.   Diffusion of Chinese Religions

    4.   From the Hearth of the Eastern Mediterranean

    5.   Diffusion of Judaism

       a.   Christianity

       b.   Diffusion of Christianity

       c.   Islam

       d.   Diffusion of Islam

       e.   Indigenous and Shamanist

       f.   The Rise of Secularism

C.   How Is Religion Seen in the Cultural Landscape?

    1.   Sacred Sites of Jerusalem

    2.   Landscapes of Hinduism and Buddhism

    3.   Landscapes of Christianity

       a.   Religious Landscapes in the United States

    4.   Landscapes of Islam

D.   What Role Does Religion Play in Political Conflicts?

    1.   Conflicts along Religious Borders

    2.   Israel and Palestine

    3.   Nigeria

    4.   The Former Yugoslavia

    5.   Northern Ireland

    6.   Religious Fundamentalism and Extremism

       a.   Christianity

       b.   Judaism

       c.   Islam

Geographic Concepts		
Religion	Confucianism	Pilgrimage
Secularism	Judaism	Sacred Sites
Monotheistic	Diaspora	Minarets
Religion	Zionism	Hajj
Polytheistic	Christianity	Interfaith
Religion	Eastern Orthodox	Boundaries
Animistic Religion	Church	Intrafaith
Universalizing	Roman Catholic	Boundaries
Religion	Church	Ethnic Cleansing
Ethnic Religion	Protestant	Activity Space
Hinduism	Islam	Religious Fundamentalism
Caste System	Sunni	Religious Extremism
Buddhism	Shi'ite	Shari'a Laws
Shintoism	Indigenous Religions	Jihad
Taoism	Shamanism	
Feng Shui	Secularism	

Step 2: Pre-Reading Activity (PRA)

Name: _____ **Period** _____ **Date** _____

Chapter Title: _____

Chapter # _____   **Pgs.** _____ **to** _____

1. Write down each of the Key Questions and the number of pages for each (go back to Step 1 of your textbook for answers).

Key Question	# of Pages

2. After looking over the key questions, looking through the outline, and reading the chapter summary, write a few sentences about what you expect to learn in general in this chapter.

_____

3. Preview the entire chapter and look at all the maps, tables, charts, and pictures. Read the captions. Briefly describe IN YOUR OWN WORDS five maps or charts.

pg. _____ _____

pg. _____ _____

pg. _____ _____

pg. _____ _____

pg. _____ _____

4. How many world maps are there in this chapter? _____ (Go to the Student Companion Website and print out the World Map Region Worksheets needed for this chapter.)

5. Read the Field Note introduction of the chapter and list five specific facts you learned.

_____

_____

_____

_____

_____

_____

_____

_____

_____

_____

_____

6. Go to Step 1 and look at the Geographic Concepts. Create a list of terms you think you know and terms you need to know.

I THINK I KNOW	I NEED TO LEARN

Step 3: Chapter 7 Guided Worksheet (Created by Parisa Watson)

Name: _____ **Period** _____ **Date** _____

Directions: As you read the chapter, fill in the blanks on the guided worksheet.

FIELD NOTE—DYING AND RESURRECTING

1. From Leningrad to Moscow there was evidence of _____ on the landscape. There were a multitude of _____ in ruins.
2. Culturally, the Soviet Union also espoused an official policy of _____.
3. In remote corners of the Soviet Union, _____ was practiced.
4. When the Soviet Union _____ in 1991, Russians proved they had not forgotten their faith. The Russian _____ church revived and _____ were rebuilt and opened.

WHAT IS RELIGION, AND WHAT ROLE DOES IT PLAY IN CULTURE?

5. _____ is an extraordinarily difficult concept to define. The indifference to or rejection of formal religion is known as _____. _____ is an area where many of these countries are located.

WHERE DID THE MAJOR RELIGIONS OF THE WORLD ORIGINATE, AND HOW DO RELIGIONS DIFFUSE?

6. _____ religions worship one God, while polytheist religions maintain the belief in _____ Gods. _____ religions are centered on the belief that objects such as mountains, boulders, rivers, and trees contain spirits and should therefore be revered.
7. _____ was the first monotheistic religion and was located in Southwest Asia.
8. _____ religions actively seek converts.
9. Name three universalizing religions: _____, _____, and _____.
10. In an _____ religion adherents are born into the faith and converts are not actively sought. They tend to be spatially concentrated with the exception of _____ whose adherents are widely scattered as a result of forced migration.
11. _____ ranks third in terms of number of followers. It has no one official book. It is one of the oldest religions and began over _____ years ago. It began in the _____ River Valley, which is located in the present-day country of _____.
12. Some define Hinduism as _____ because of the presence of many gods. However, many Hindus define their religion as _____.

13. The Hindu religion is not centrally _____. It does not have a _____ or a single _____. The fundamental doctrine is _____.

14. Hinduism's doctrines are closely bound to Indian society's _____ _____.

15. Buddhism splintered from _____. The founder, _____, spoke out against the caste system. Like Christianity and Islam, it grew and diffused. There are many Buddhists in countries such as _____. Other branches of Buddhism include _____ of Xizang (Tibet).

16. Buddhism is mixed with a local religion in Japan, where _____ is found. It focuses particularly on _____ and ancestral worship.

17. Lao-Tsu is the founder of _____. It involves living in harmony with nature and gave rise to _____ _____, the art and science of organizing living spaces in order to channel the life forces that exist in nature in favorable ways. According to tradition, nothing should be done to nature without consulting the _____, people who know the desires of the powerful spirits of ancestors, dragons, tigers, and other beings.

18. _____ is mainly a philosophy of life and is found in China and East Asia with Confucius as its founder. _____ came to be revered as a spiritual leader after his death. From his writings and sayings emerged the _____ _____, a set of 13 texts that became the focus of education in China for 2000 years.

19. The diffusion of Chinese religions even within China has been tempered by the _____ _____ efforts to suppress religion in the country.

20. _____ grew out of the belief system of the Jews, one of the several nomadic Semitic tribes living in Southwest Asia about 4000 years ago. The roots of the religion lie in the teachings of _____, who united his people to worship _____ God.

21. After the fall of the Roman Empire, the scattering of Jews is referred to as the _____. The Jews who went north into Central Europe came to be known as _____, and the Jews who scattered across North Africa and the Iberian Peninsula were called _____.

22. The idea of a homeland for the Jews in Israel is referred to as _____.

23. _____ can be traced back to the same hearth in the Mediterranean as Judaism, and like Judaism, Christianity stems from a single founder, _____.

24. The three branches of Christianity are _____, _____ _____ and _____ _____. List where each branch is found:
_____.

25. _____ is the largest and globally the most widely dispersed religion. _____ _____ is the largest sect of Christianity.

26. _____ is the youngest of the main religions and can be traced to Muhammad.

27. Adherents to Islam are required to observe the _____ _____. Islam forbids _____, _____ and _____. People build _____ to observe the Friday prayer and use for social gatherings.

28. The two main branches are _____ and _____. Most _____ are concentrated in Iran.

29. The hearth of the religion is _____ _____ (Figure 7.16).

30. It ranks ___ in terms of number of followers. It is the _____ growing of the world's major religions.

31. The largest Muslim country is actually outside the Middle East in the Southeast Asian country of _____.

32. An _____ religion is local in scope, usually has a reverence for nature, and is passed down through family units and groups.

33. _____ is a community faith in which people follow their _____ a religious leader, teacher, healer, and visionary. List where it is found (go back to Figure 7.6): _____.

HOW IS RELIGION SEEN IN THE CULTURAL LANDSCAPE?

34. Religion marks cultural landscapes with houses of worship such as

_____.

35. When adherents voluntarily travel to a religious site to pay respects or participate in a ritual at a site, the act of travel is called a _____.

36. _____ _____ are places or spaces that people infuse with religious meaning.

37. The ancient city of _____ is sacred to Jews, Christians, and Muslims. The most sacred site for the Jews is the _____ _____. For Christians, the Church of the Holy Sepulchre maintains the _____ that Jesus rose from the dead on Easter. The _____ of the _____ is sacred for Muslims as it is the site at which Muhammad arrived from Mecca and then ascended into heaven.

38. Hindus believe that the erection of a _____ bestows merit on the builder and will be rewarded. As a result, the Hindu cultural landscape is dotted with countless _____.

39. When Buddha became enlightened, he sat under a large _____ tree. Buddhists also have shrines called _____ that are bell-shaped structures. In terms of the dead, Hindus believe in _____.

40. The cultural landscape of Christianity includes items such as _____.

41. In the United States, the _____ are located in the South, the _____ in the upper Midwest, and the _____ in Utah and surrounding areas.

42. Minarets and mosques are associated with the _____ faith.

43. The Muslim pilgrimage to Mecca is known as the _____.

WHAT ROLE DOES RELIGION PLAY IN POLITICAL CONFLICTS?

44. _____ are boundaries between the world's major faiths. Examples:

_____.

45. _____ are boundaries within a single faith. Examples:

_____.

46. The region of _____ and _____ is home to one of the most contentious religious conflicts in the world today. The _____ _____ voted to partition Palestine.

47. In Nigeria, the _____ religion dominates in the north, and _____ dominates in the south.

48. A number of religious and linguistic fault lines run through the _____ Peninsula. The Slovenians and Croats in the west are _____ and the Serbians and Montenegrans in the east and south are _____ _____.

49. The term _____ _____ came into use to describe the ouster of Bosnian Muslims and others from their homes and lands—and sometimes their slaughter.

50. Today _____ _____ and Great Britain (which includes England, Scotland, and Wales) form the United Kingdom of Great Britain and Northern Ireland (UK). In the face of worsening conflict, Catholics and _____ in Northern Ireland increasingly distanced their lives and homes from one another.

51. _____ _____ is when religious leaders and their followers are seeking to return to the basics of their faith. It is borne out of frustration over the perceived breakdown of society's morals and _____, lack of religious authority, failure to achieve economic goals, a _____ of a sense of local control, or a sense of violation of a religion's core territory.

52. _____ _____ is when religious fundamentalism is taken to the point of violence.

53. Mel Gibson belongs to the _____ _____ _____, which does not recognize the Pope. Judaism has _____ sects. The most conservative sect is _____. The _____ and _____ _____ are followers of the late American-born Israeli Rabbi Meir Kahane and is an extremist group.

54. _____ is another name used for Islamic holy war and is sought by Islamic extremists.

Step 4: Remember to fill out World Region Map Sheets.

Go to the Student Companion Website to print out the sheets: www.wiley.com/college/ Fouberg

Step 5: Practice Quiz

Chapter 7: Religion

Multiple Choice Questions

1. The vote to partition Palestine was taken by
   A. Israel
   B. the United Nations
   C. Britain
   D. the Ottoman Empire
   E. League of Nations

2.   The ideology of Zionism has as its goal
     A.   the merger of Judaism with other religions
     B.   the merger of the three modern divisions of Judaism
     C.   a homeland for the Jewish people
     D.   the elimination of the Orthodox division within the faith
     E.   the search for the true Mount Zion where the Ten Commandments were revealed

3.   The youngest major religion is
     A.   Hinduism
     B.   Judaism
     C.   Islam
     D.   Christianity
     E.   Buddhism

4.   Modern-day Shi'a Islam dominates a region centered on
     A.   Pakistan and Afghanistan
     B.   Saudi Arabia and Oman
     C.   Armenia and Azerbaijan
     D.   Indonesia and Malaysia
     E.   Iran and Iraq

5.   The Hajj, one of the "pillars of Islam," is
     A.   charitable giving
     B.   fasting during the holy month
     C.   the veil worn by Muslim women
     D.   the pilgrimage to Mecca
     E.   the five daily prayers

6.   The world's largest Islamic state with regard to population is
     A.   Iran
     B.   Pakistan
     C.   Egypt
     D.   Indonesia
     E.   India

7.   The Jews of Central Europe are known as
     A.   Ashkenazim
     B.   Sephardim
     C.   Zionists
     D.   Orthodox
     E.   Reformed

8. The faith that is most widely dispersed over the world is
    A. Christianity
    B. Islam
    C. Shamanism
    D. Buddhism
    E. Baha'i Faith

9. Sikhism is a small compromise religion that arose from the confrontation between
    Hinduism and
    A. Buddhism
    B. Jainism
    C. Christianity
    D. British colonial officials
    E. Islam

10. Zoroastrianism is similar to Islam and Christianity in that it is
    A. a world religion
    B. monotheistic
    C. a missionary religion
    D. polytheistic
    E. a desert faith in origin

11. The diaspora of the Jews resulted from
    A. Moses' decision to leave Egypt
    B. the Arab-Israeli conflict
    C. the holocaust
    D. the Roman destruction of Jerusalem
    E. disagreements between the Sadducees and the Pharisees

12. Which is NOT a feature of Islamic sacred architecture?
    A. minarets
    B. adoption of Roman models of design
    C. influenced by the architecture of other civilizations
    D. geometric and calligraphic ornamentation
    E. frescoes depicting the life of the prophet

CHAPTER 8:
POLITICAL GEOGRAPHY

The Five Steps to Chapter Success Checklist

Step 1: Read the Chapter Summary below, preview the Key Questions, the Chapter Outline, and the terms of the chapter.

Step 2: Complete the Pre-Reading Activity (PRA) for this chapter.

Step 3: Read the chapter and complete the guided worksheet.

Step 4: As you read the chapter, complete World Region Map Sheets for every world map. Go to the Student Companion Website to print out the WRMS.

Step 5: Take an AP-style Practice Quiz.

STEP 1: Chapter Summary, Key Questions, Chapter Outline and Geographic Concepts

Chapter Summary

We tend to take the state for granted, but the modern state idea is less than 400 years old. The idea and ideal of the nation-state have diffused around the globe in the wake of colonialism and the emergence of the modern international legal order.

The state may seem natural and permanent, but it is not. New states are being recognized, and existing states are vulnerable to destructive forces. How long can this way of politically organizing space last?

As we look to arrangements beyond the state, we can turn to the global scale and consider what places the global world economy most affects, shapes, and benefits. In the next chapter, we study global cities with major links in the world economy. Global cities dominate their surroundings and connect with each other across the world in many ways that transcend the state.

Key Questions

Field Note: Independence Is Better Than Servitude	249–252
1. How is space politically organized into states and nations?	252–264
2. How do states spatially organize their governments?	264–272
3. How are boundaries established, and why do boundary disputes occur?	272–275
4. How does the study of geopolitics help us understand the world?	275–278
5. What are supranational organizations, and what are their implications for the state?	278–286

Chapter 8 Outline

A. How Is Space Politically Organized Into States and Nations?
   1. The Modern State Idea
   2. Nations
   3. Nation-State
   4. Multistate Nations, Multinational States, and Stateless Nations
   5. European Colonialism and the Diffusion of the Nation-State Model
   6. Construction of the Capitalist World Economy
   7. World-Systems and Political Power
   8. The Enduring Impact of the Nation-State Ideal

B. How Do States Spatially Organize Their Governments?
   1. Form of Government
   2. Devolution
      a. Ethnocultural Devolutionary Movements
      b. Economic Devolutionary Forces
      c. Territorial Influences on Devolution
   3. Electoral Geography

C. How Are Boundaries Established, and Why Do Boundary Disputes Occur?
   1. Establishing Boundaries
   2. Types of Boundaries
   3. Boundaries Disputes

D. How Does the Study of Geopolitics Help Us Understand the World?
   1. Classic Geopolitics
   2. The German School
   3. The British/American School
   4. Influence of Geopoliticians on Politics
   5. Critical Geopolitics
   6. Geopolitical World Order

E. What Are Supranational Organizations, and What Are Their Implications for the State?
   1. From League of Nations to United Nations
   2. Regional Supranational Organizations
   3. The European Union
   4. How Does Supranationalism Affect the State?

Geographic Concepts		
Political Geography	Colonialism	Territorial Representation
State	Scale	Reapportionment
Territory	World-Systems Theory	Splitting
Territoriality	Capitalism	Majority-Minority Districts
Sovereignty	Commodification	Gerrymandering
Territorial Integrity	Core	Boundary
Mercantilism	Periphery	Geometric Boundary
Peace of Westphalia	Semiperiphery	Physical-Political Boundary
Nation	Ability	Heartland Theory
Nation-State	Centripetal	Critical Geopolitics
Democracy	Centrifugal	Unilateralism
Multinational State	Unitary	Supranational Organization
Multistate Nation	Federal	Deterritorialization
Stateless Nation	Devolution	Reterritorialization

Step 2: Pre-Reading Activity (PRA)

Name: _____   **Period** _____   **Date** _____

Chapter Title: _____

Chapter # _____   **Pgs.** _____ **to** _____

1. Write down each of the Key Questions and the number of pages for each (go back to Step 1 of your textbook for answers).

Key Question	# of Pages

2. After looking over the key questions, looking through the outline, and reading the chapter summary, write a few sentences about what you expect to learn in general in this chapter.

3.   Preview the entire chapter and look at all the maps, tables, charts, and pictures. Read the captions. Briefly describe IN YOUR OWN WORDS five maps or charts.

pg. _____ _____

pg. _____ _____

pg. _____ _____

pg. _____ _____

pg. _____ _____

4.   How many world maps are there in this chapter? _____ (Go to the Student Companion Website and print out the World Map Region Worksheets needed for this chapter.)

5.   Read the Field Note introduction of the chapter and list five specific facts you learned.

_____

_____

_____

_____

_____

_____

_____

_____

_____

_____

_____

6.   Go to Step 1 and look at the Geographic Concepts. Create a list of terms you think you know and terms you need to know.

I THINK I KNOW	I NEED TO LEARN

Step 3: Chapter 8 Guided Worksheet (Created by Parisa Watson)

Name: _____ **Period** _____ **Date** _____

Directions: As you read the chapter, fill in the blanks on the guided worksheet.

FIELD NOTE—-INDEPENDENCE IS BETTER THAN SOLITUDE

1. Ghana, the first _____ African colony to become independent, gained its independence in _____. A wave of decolonization swept through Africa in the _____, fueled by the hope that decolonization would bring political and economic _____.

2. Each country had to deal with significant problems after independence, including a mixture of peoples, cultures, _____ and _____ that were grouped within single political units during the colonial period.

HOW IS SPACE POLITICALLY ORGANIZED INTO STATES AND NATIONS?

3. _____ _____ is the study of the political organization of the world. At the global scale, we have a world divided into individual _____ which are commonly called _____.

4. A _____ is a politically organized territory with a permanent population, a defined territory, and a government. To be a state, an entity must be _____ as such by other states.

5. Today on a map, there are more than _____ countries and territories.

6. Central to the state are the concepts of _____ and territoriality. Stuart Elden pointed out that the modern concept of territoriality arose in early modern _____ as a system of political units came into being with fixed, distinct boundaries and some type of government. Robert Sack defined _____ as "the attempt by an individual or group to affect, influence, or control people, phenomena, and relationships, by delimiting and asserting control over a geographic area."

7. Today, the concept of territoriality is tied to the concept of _____ as the behavior implies an expression of control over a _____. Under international law, states are _____, and they have the right to defend their territorial _____ against incursion from others.

8. The emerging political state was accompanied by _____, which led to the accumulation of wealth through plunder, colonization, and the protection of home industries and foreign markets.

9. The Peace of Westphalia marks _____, which was negotiated in the year _____.

10. The popular media and press often use the words _____, _____ and _____ interchangeably, but the word _____ is distinct.

11. A group of people who think of themselves as one based on a sense of shared culture and history, and who seek some degree of political autonomy is defined as

    _____.

12. When a nation and state occupy the same territory, it is known as a _____. The goal of creating _____ dates back to the French Revolution. The Revolution initially promoted _____, the idea that the people, the _____, have the ultimate say over what happens within a state.

13. People with a sense of belonging to a particular nation _____ reside within a single state's borders. Nearly every state in the world is a _____ _____, a state with more than one _____ inside its borders. When a nation stretches across borders and across states, the nation is called a _____ _____.

14. Some nations do not have a state, they are _____ _____. The _____ are an example. A much larger stateless nation is the _____ whose population covers parts of six states.

15. Europe exported its concepts of state, sovereignty, and desire for nation-states to much of the rest of the world through two waves of _____. The colonizing parties met at the _____ _____ and arbitrarily laid out the colonial map of _____ without regard to indigenous cultural or political arrangements.

16. During the heyday of _____, the imperial powers exercised ruthless control over their domains and organized them for maximum economic exploitation. Colonizers organized the flows of _____ _____ for their own benefit.

17. _____ and _____ were the countries with the most African colonies (Figure 8.8).

18. The world-systems theory views the world as much more than the _____ _____ of the world's states. According to Wallerstein, the development of a world economy began with _____ exchange around 1450. _____ means that in the world economy, individuals, corporations, and states produce goods and services that are exchanged for profit.

19. Lastly, the world-systems theorists see the world as a three-tiered structure: the _____, _____ and _____. The _____ is where one is most likely to find higher levels of education, _____ salaries, and more technology and generate more _____ in the world economy. The _____ more commonly has lower levels of education, _____ salaries, and less technology and are associated with a more _____ position in the world economy. Places where both core and periphery processes are occurring are called _____.

HOW DO STATES SPATIALLY ORGANIZE THEIR GOVERNMENTS?

20. A _____ force helps unite people within a state, while _____ _____ are divisive forces in a state.

21. Highly centralized governments in which the power is focused on the capital city are called
    _____ governments.
22. The _____ system gives much more control to regions than the central
    government.
23. _____ is the movement of power from the central government to regional
    governments within the state.
24. Nigeria's _____ _____ are an example of the federal system.
25. _____ is the movement of power from the central government to regional
    governments within the state. It does not necessarily fuel greater calls for _____.
    Nations within states can, instead, call for autonomy within the borders of the _____. In
    the UK, Scotland established its own _____ in 1997.
26. Cite at least three examples of devolution throughout the world (Figure 8.14).

    _____

27. The domain in which electoral geographers can have the most concrete influence is in the
    drawing of _____ _____. The U.S. Constitution establishes a system of _____
    _____. In the Senate, each major territorial unit gets two representatives, and in the
    House of Representatives, members are elected from territorially defined districts based on
    _____.
28. The Constitution requires a census every _____ years to enumerate the population and
    reapportion the representatives accordingly. When districts are moved according to
    population shift, it is known as _____.
29. Majority-minority districts are packed districts in which the majority of the population is
    from the _____.
30. Redistricting for advantage is called _____.

HOW ARE BOUNDARIES ESTABLISHED, AND WHY DO BOUNDARY DISPUTES OCCUR?

31. The territories of individual states are separated by international boundaries, often referred
    to as _____. They may appear on maps as _____ lines or turn and conform with
    rivers and curves of hills and valleys. But a boundary is more than a _____, far more than
    a fence or wall on the ground.
32. A _____ between states is actually a _____ plane that cuts through the rocks
    below and the airspace above, dividing one state from another.
33. _____ boundaries are drawn using a grid system such as latitude and longitude or
    township and range. The boundary between the countries of _____ and _____ is an
    example of this, along with many of the boundaries of _____.
34. _____ _____ are boundaries that follow an agreed-upon feature in the
    natural landscape, such as the center point of a river or the crest of a mountain range. The
    _____ _____ is an example of this, dividing the United States and Mexico.

35. Boundary disputes can take four principal forms: _____, _____, _____, and
    _____.

36. _____ boundary disputes focus on the legal language of the boundary agreement, such
    as the median line of a _____. _____ boundary disputes center on the delimitation
    and possibly demarcation of the boundary. _____ boundary disputes involve
    neighbors who differ over the way their border should function. An example would be
    _____ functions in terms of migration. _____ boundary disputes are common as
    the search for resources intensifies. _____ reserves and _____ supplies are two
    common examples of this dispute.

HOW DOES THE STUDY OF GEOPOLITICS HELP US UNDERSTAND THE WORLD?

37. _____ is the interplay among geography, power, politics, and international
    relations on the Earth's surface.

38. Classical geopolitics of the late nineteenth and early twentieth centuries generally fit into two
    camps: the _____ school and the _____ school.

39. Ratzel's organic theory said that the state resembles a biological organism that needs
    _____ just as an organisms needs _____. Such nourishment is provided by the
    acquisition of _____ that provide adequate space for members of the state. This theory is
    most associated with the philosophy of _____ _____.

40. _____ proposed the heartland theory, stating that whoever rules the heartland
    rules the world island and the world. The heartland includes the region of
    _____.

WHAT ARE SUPRANATIONAL ORGANIZATIONS, AND WHAT ARE THEIR IMPLICATIONS FOR THE STATE?

41. A supranational organization is an entity comprised of _____ or more states for mutual
    benefit.

42. The modern beginnings of the supranational movement can be traced to conferences
    following _____ _____ _____. After World War II, states formed a new organization to
    foster international security and cooperation: the _____ _____. By participating in the
    UN, states commit to internationally approved standards of _____. States still violate
    standards, but such violations can lead to collective action such as _____ sanctions or
    Security Council supported _____ _____.

43. From the Marshall Plan came the Organization for European Economic Cooperation
    (_____). Eventually, in 1958, this led to the _____ _____ _____. Their
    success encouraged others to join and the organization became known as the _____
    _____. In 1992, the 12 members initiated a program of cooperation and unification that
    led to the formal establishment of a _____ _____. In the late 1990s the EU began
    negotiations for the establishment of a single currency—the _____. Under the rules of
    the _____, the richer countries have to _____ the poorer ones.

44. Some people would like to see Turkey join the EU, but the conflict between _____ and _____ over Cyprus is an issue.
45. The EU is an example of a _____ _____.
46. List a supranationational organization in North America _____, South America _____, Asia _____, Europe _____.

Step 4: Remember to fill out World Region Map Sheets.

Go to the Student Companion Website to print out the sheets: www.wiley.com/college/Fouberg

Step 5: Practice Quiz

Chapter 8: Political Geography

Multiple Choice Questions

1. One move by the old League of Nations that would have a critical impact in the second half of the twentieth century involved
   A. maritime boundaries
   B. refugee questions
   C. atmospheric boundaries
   D. mineral resources underlying two or more countries
   E. ignored global warning

2. The United Nations is not a world government, but in recent years individual states have asked the UN to do a number of different things, the most expensive of which is
   A. creating a common global currency
   B. monitoring elections
   C. providing for refugees
   D. setting maritime boundaries
   E. peacekeeping

3. The European Union's future expansion into the Muslim realm by the inclusion of _____ is highly controversial and strongly opposed by Greece.
   A. Saudi Arabia
   B. Bosnia
   C. Algeria
   D. Turkey
   E. Iraq

4. Sir Halford Mackinder developed what would become known as the heartland theory, which suggested that interior Eurasia contained a critical "pivot area" that would generate a state capable of world domination. The key to the area according to Mackinder was
    A. natural protection
    B. distance
    C. natural resources
    D. eastern Europe
    E. the Russian steppe

5. The movement of power from the central government to regional governments is referred to as
    A. revolution
    B. pluralism
    C. supranationalism
    D. devolution
    E. decentralization

6. The boundaries of independent African states were drawn at the Berlin Conference and were essentially drawn along
    A. arbitrary lines
    B. ethnic lines
    C. religious lines
    D. ecological lines
    E. linguistic lines

7. Yugoslavia was a prime example of a
    A. multistate nation
    B. nation-state
    C. stateless nation
    D. unitary state
    E. multination state

8. The present number of countries and territories in the world is approximately
    A. 400
    B. 350
    C. 300
    D. 200
    E. 100

9. The view of human territorial behavior implies an expression of control over space and time. This control is closely related to the concept of
    A. nationhood
    B. colonialism
    C. sovereignty
    D. warfare
    E. hegemony

10. Nigeria is a state with a federal system of government. This fact is reflected in the adoption of _____ law in the states of the Muslim North.
    A. British Common
    B. Nigerian Federal
    C. Sharia
    D. local tribal
    E. states' rights

11. In 1943, Mackinder wrote about his concerns over the potential of Stalin's control of the countries of eastern Europe. His views led to the development of the United States' containment policy and to the establishment of
    A. the League of Nations
    B. COMECON
    C. NATO
    D. the Berlin Wall
    E. the United Nations

12. Listed among the challenges to the state in the twenty-first century are all the following EXCEPT
    A. nuclear weapons
    B. economic globalization
    C. increased cultural communication
    D. terrorism in the name of religion
    E. the United Nations

CHAPTER 9:
URBAN GEOGRAPHY

The Five Steps to Chapter Success Checklist

Step 1: Read the Chapter Summary below, preview the Key Questions, the Chapter Outline, and
    the terms of the chapter.
Step 2: Complete the Pre-Reading Activity (PRA) for this chapter.
Step 3: Read the chapter and complete the guided worksheet.
Step 4: As you read the chapter, complete World Region Map Sheets for every world map.
    Go to the Student Companion Website to print out the WRMS.
Step 5: Take an AP-style Practice Quiz.

STEP 1: Chapter Summary, Key Questions, Chapter Outline, and Geographic Concepts

Chapter Summary

The city is an ever-changing cultural landscape, its layers reflecting grand plans by governments, impassioned pursuits by individuals, economic decisions by corporations, and processes of globalization. Geographers who study cities have a multitude of topics to examine. From gentrification to tear-downs, from favelas to McMansions, from spaces of production to spaces of consumption, from ancient walls to gated communities, cities have so much in common and yet each has its own pulse, its own feel, its own spatial structure, its own set of realities. The pulse of the city is undoubtedly created by the peoples and cultures who live there. For it is the people, whether working independently or as part of global institutions, who continuously create and re-create the city and its geography.

Key Questions

Field Note: Ghosts of Detroit?	288–290
1. When and why did people start living in cities?	291–304
2. Where are cities located and why?	304–308
3. How are cities organized, and how do they function?	308–314
4. How do people shape cities?	315–328
5. What role do cities play in globalization?	329–331

Chapter 9 Outline

A. When and Why Did People Start Living in Cities?
    1.   The Hearths of Urbanization
    2.   The Role of the Ancient City in Society
    3.   Diffusion of Urbanization
    4.   Greek Cities
    5.   Roman Cities
    6.   Urban Growth after Greece and Rome
    7.   Site and Situation during European Exploration
    8.   The Second Urban Revolution
    9.   A Second Agricultural Revolution
    10. The Chaotic Industrial City

B. Where Are Cities Locate and Why?
    1.   Rank and Size in the Urban Matrix
    2.   Central Place Theory
    3.   Hexagonal Hinterlands
    4.   Central Places Today

C. How Are Cities Organized, and How Do They Function?
    1.   Models of the City
    2.   Functional Zones
    3.   Modeling the North American City
    4.   Modeling the Cities of the Global Periphery and Semiperiphery
    5.   The South American City
    6.   The African City
    7.   The Southeast Asian City

D. How Do People Shape Cities?
    1.   Shaping Cities in the Global Periphery and Semiperiphery
    2.   Shaping Cities in the Global Core
    3.   Urban Sprawl and New Urbanism
    4.   Gated Communities
    5.   Ethnic Neighborhoods in the European City
    6.   Government Policy and Immigrant Accommodation
    7.   Ethnic Neighborhoods in the Global Periphery and Semiperiphery City
    8.   Power and Electricity
    9.   The Informal Economy
    10. From Colonial to Global CBD

E. What Role Do Cities Play in Globalization?
    1.   Cities as Spaces of Consumption

Geographic Concepts		
Central Business District (CBD)	Site	Shantytowns
Synekism	Situation	Disamenity Sector
Urban	Urban Morphology	Mcgee Model
City	Functional Zonation	Zoning Laws
Agricultural Village	Forum	Redlining
Agricultural Surplus	Trade Area	Blockbusting
Social Stratification	Rank-Size Rule	Commercialization
Leadership Class	Primate City	Gentrification
First Urban Revolution	Central Place Theory	Teardowns
Mesopotamia	Sun Phenomenon	McMansions
Nile River Valley	Zone	Urban Sprawl
Indus River Valley	Central City	New Urbanism
Huang He and Wei River Valleys	Suburb	Gated Communities
Mesoamerica	Suburbanization	Informal Economy
Peru	Concentric Zone Model	World City
Secondary Hearth	Edge Cities	Spaces of Consumption
Acropolis	Megacities	
Agora	Griffin-Ford Model	

Step 2: Pre-Reading Activity (PRA)

Name: _____   **Period** _____   **Date** _____

Chapter Title: _____

Chapter # _____   **Pgs.** _____ **to** _____

1. Write down each of the Key Questions and the number of pages for each (go back to Step 1
    of your textbook for answers).

Key Question	# of Pages

2.   After looking over the Key Questions, looking through the outline, and reading the chapter summary, write a few sentences about what you expect to learn in general in this chapter.

3.   Preview the entire chapter and look at all the maps, tables, charts, and pictures. Read the captions. Briefly describe IN YOUR OWN WORDS five maps or charts.

pg. _____ _____

pg. _____ _____

pg. _____ _____

pg. _____ _____

pg. _____ _____

4.   How many world maps are there in this chapter? _____ (Go to the Student Companion Website and print out the World Map Region Worksheets needed for this chapter.)

5.   Read the Field Note introduction of the chapter and list five specific facts you learned.

_____

_____

_____

_____

_____

_____

_____

_____

_____

_____

6.   Go to Step 1 and look at the Geographic Concepts. Create a list of terms you think you know and terms you need to know.

I THINK I KNOW	I NEED TO LEARN

Step 3: Chapter 9 Guided Worksheet (Created by Parisa Watson)

Name: _____ **Period** _____ **Date** _____

Directions: As you read the chapter, fill in the blanks on the guided worksheet.

FIELD NOTE—GHOSTS OF DETROIT?

1. The _____ is the downtown or concentration of business or commerce.
2. The population of Detroit rose and fell with the _____ industry. The population peaked at _____ million in 1950, but the 2010 census shows the city's population falling to _____.

WHEN AND WHY DID PEOPLE START LIVING IN CITIES?

3. Worldwide, today more people live in _____ areas than in rural areas. _____ refers to the central city and surrounding areas. For most of human history, the world was largely _____. The _____ _____ in the mid-1700s marks the time when urbanization exploded for the first time.
4. _____ are the centers of political power and industrial might, _____ _____ and technological innovation, artistic achievement and medical advancements. They are anchors and instigators of modern _____. A _____ is an agglomeration of people and buildings clustered together to serve as a center of _____, _____ and _____.
5. In the modern world, _____ can happen quite quickly. Archaeological evidence indicates that people established the first cities about _____ years ago.
6. The switch from _____ and _____ to agriculture occurred prior to urbanization. Agricultural villages were relatively _____ in size and in population. Everyone living in an _____ _____ was involved in agriculture at the most basic level.
7. Two components enabled cities to stabilize and grow: _____ _____ and _____ _____. The _____ _____ or urban elite, consisted of a group of decision makers and organizers who controlled the resources, and often the lives of others. They also controlled the _____ supply.
8. The innovation of the city is called the _____ _____ _____ and it occurred independently in six separate hearths. The first urban hearth is _____, located

between the rivers _____ and _____. _____ dominated the urban landscape.

9.   The second urban hearth of urbanization is the _____ _____ _____. The third urban hearth is the _____ _____ _____. The fourth urban hearth arose around the confluence of the _____ _____ and _____ _____ of present-day China. The cities had an inner wall with _____ and palaces for the leadership class. Chronologically, the fifth urban hearth is _____. Many cities centered on religious _____. The most recent archaeological evidence establishes _____ as the sixth urban hearth, chronologically.

10.   Ancient cities not only were centers of religion and power, but also served as _____ nodes. By modern standards, the ancient city was not _____. The cities of Mesopotamia and the Nile Valley may have had between _____ and _____ inhabitants.

11.   Greece is more accurately described as a _____ _____ of urbanization. The largest city of Athens had an estimated _____ inhabitants.

12.   An _____ was the high point of the Greek city, while the _____ was the name for market.

13.   The Romans had a number of large settlements ranging from small _____ to large _____. The Romans linked these places with an extensive _____ network that included hundreds of miles of _____.

14.   The _____ of a city is based on its role in the larger, surrounding context. It is its _____ location, its place in the region and the world around it.

15.   The _____ _____ of a city is the layout, its physical form and structure. When we add the purpose or use of buildings to the map of the morphology of a city, we reveal the _____ _____ of the city. It reveals how different areas or segments of a city serve different _____. The _____ was the focal point of Roman life. It included the _____, a much grander version of the Greek theatre.

16.   During the last decades of the eighteenth century, the _____ _____ began in Great Britain. Before the second urban revolution could take place, a second revolution in _____ was necessary. With industrialization, cities became unregulated jumbles of activity. Cities of the British Midlands became known as _____ _____.

WHERE ARE CITIES LOCATED AND WHY?

17.   Site and _____ help explain why cities were planned and why cities thrive or _____. In studying the size of cities and distances between them, urban geographers explored the _____ _____ of different sized cities.

18.   The _____ _____ _____ holds that in model urban hierarchy, the population of a city or town will be inversely proportional to its rank in the hierarchy. According to the rank size rule, if the largest city is 12 million, the next will be _____, the third _____ and the fourth _____.

19. The rank size rule does not apply in all countries, especially one with a _____ _____. A _____ _____ is a "country's leading city, always disproportionately large and exceptionally expressive of national capacity and feeling."

20. _____ created the central place theory. His assumptions include the following: _____. Within a trade area of the largest central place, a series of larger _____ would provide functions to several smaller places. The central place theory is in the shape of a _____.

21. The _____ _____ phenomenon stresses that central place notions still have a role in explaining current developments. In this phenomenon, millions of Americans move from the _____ to the _____ and _____.

HOW ARE CITIES ORGANIZED, AND HOW DO THEY FUNCTION?

22. One way to conceptualize the layout of cities is through the _____ that illustrate the structures of cities. Each model of the city, regardless of the region, is a study of _____ _____—the division of the city into certain regions (_____) for certain purposes (_____).

23. The term _____ is typically preceded by a descriptor that conveys the purpose of that area of the city. The term _____ _____ refers to the urban area that is not suburban. A _____ is an outlying, functionally uniform part of an urban area and is often adjacent to the central city. Suburbanization is the process by which lands that were previously outside of the _____ environment become _____.

24. Ernest Burgess made the _____ _____ _____ after the city of _____. It is comprised of _____ concentric rings, defined by their function. At the center is the _____, zone 2 is characterized by residential _____ and encroachment by business and light manufacturing. Zone 3 comprises closely spaced but adequate homes occupied by a _____ collar labor force. Zone 4 consists of _____ residences, and zone 5 is the _____ ring.

25. Homer Hoyt created the _____ model. He focused mainly on _____ patterns, explaining where the wealthy in a _____ choose to live. He argued that the city grows _____ from the center. The zones could be shaped like a piece of _____.

26. _____ ____ _____ proposed the multiple nuclei model in the 1940s, with the _____ losing its dominance.

27. Most urban geographers think these models are too _____ to describe the modern city.

28. Cities that are located near freeways and intersections are called _____ _____.

29. Primate cities in developing countries are called _____ when the city has a large population, a vast territorial extend, rapid in-migration, and a strained, inadequate infrastructure.

30. The Latin American city model is referred to as the _____ model. It consists of a _____ in the center.

31. _____ are unplanned developments of dwellings made of scrap and cardboard, and develop around cities.
32. The South American city also has a disamenity and *periférico* that can be home to _____ and _____ _____.
33. The African city has _____ CBDs and has _____ _____ _____ in its outer ring.
34. The Southeast Asian city has a _____ _____ instead of a CBD and is referred to as the _____ model. The alien commercial zone is dominated by _____ merchants.

HOW DO PEOPLE SHAPE CITIES?

35. Through _____ _____, cities define areas of the city and designate the kinds of development allowed in each zone. Portland, Oregon, is often described as the best planned city because it is a _____ _____ with office buildings and residential zones in close proximity to encourage _____, biking and public transportation. _____, Texas is the only city that does not have zoning laws.
36. Many of the most populous cities in the world are located in the _____ prosperous parts of the world, including places like _____. Cities in poorer parts of the world generally lack enforceable _____ _____.
37. Redlining involves financial institutions refusing to give _____ to minorities looking for housing in _____ _____.
38. Blockbusting occurred when _____ tried to get whites to sell their homes under the guise that _____ were moving into the neighborhood.
39. When cities or individuals buy up and rehabilitate housing, raising the value of the neighborhood, it is called _____.
40. After a home is torn down, newer homes are sometimes referred to as _____.
41. A major problem with cities involving unrestricted growth and congestion is called _____ _____. To counter this problem, a number of architects, urban planners, and developers outlined an urban design vision known as _____ _____. In this development, urban revitalization and suburban reform create _____ neighborhoods with a diversity of housing and jobs.
42. _____ _____ are fenced-in neighborhoods with controlled access gates for people and automobiles.
43. European cities are much older than American cities and were therefore designed for _____ and horse traffic. They are then typically more _____, densely populated and walkable than American _____.
44. The illegal activities of an economy that can't be recorded as income such as drugs and under the table money are part of the _____ economy.
45. _____ cities function at the global scale, beyond the reach of the state borders, functioning as the service centers of the world economy.

Step 4: Remember to fill out World Region Map Sheets.

Go to the Student Companion Website to print out the sheets: www.wiley.com/college/ Fouberg

Step 5: Practice Quiz

Chapter 9: Urban Geography

Multiple Choice Questions

1. Ethnic neighborhoods in European cities may reflect migrants from
   A. eastern Europe
   B. poor Mediterranean Europe
   C. former colonies
   D. Latin America
   E. Sunbelt cities

2. Segregation in the United States was reinforced by the financial practice known as
   A. redlining
   B. community block grants
   C. land-use zoning
   D. tax-increment financing
   E. microcredit

3. In core area cities, the practice of buying up and rehabilitating deteriorating housing, which results in raising housing values and a social change in neighborhoods, is called
   A. public housing
   B. gentrification
   C. white flight
   D. urban renewal
   E. revitalization

4. The huge influx of population from rural to urban areas in peripheral or semiperipheral areas (less developed countries) finds housing in
   A. public housing
   B. edge cities
   C. deteriorating CBDs
   D. high-density apartments
   E. shantytowns

5. A structural element of many Latin American cities, the disamenity sector, is illustrated by the
    A. mall
    B. barrios or favelas
    C. commercial spine
    D. industrial park
    E. presence of Chinese

6. Which of the following is BOTH the least urbanized AND the most rapidly urbanizing realm of the world?
    A. Middle America
    B. Africa south of the Sahara
    C. East Asia
    D. South Asia
    E. the Middle East

7. In Southeast Asian cities, the alien commercial zone is dominated by
    A. American corporations
    B. European industrialists
    C. Chinese merchants
    D. Lebanese traders
    E. squatter settlements

8. The relative location of a city refers to its
    A. site
    B. situation
    C. genealogy of development
    D. approximate latitude and longitude
    E. physical characteristics

9. The manufacturing city (post-Industrial Revolution) first emerged in
    A. the British Midlands
    B. central Italy
    C. the French coastal region
    D. the Ruhr
    E. Appalachia

10. In which of the following regions did urbanization develop first?
    A. Mesopotamia
    B. Nile River Valley
    C. Indus River Valley
    D. China
    E. Mesoamerica

11. The layout of a city, the physical form and structure, is referred to as
    A. zoning
    B. urban grid
    C. city plan
    D. urban street pattern
    E. urban morphology

12. A hinterland reveals the _____ of each settlement.
    A. total population
    B. working population
    C. economic reach
    D. aggregate purchasing power
    E. quality of agricultural land

13. Paris and Mexico City are many times larger than the second-ranked city in their respective countries. Their disproportionate size illustrates
    A. the concept of the primate city
    B. the fact that capital cities are always very large
    C. the rank-size rule
    D. the effects of suburbanization
    E. urban power structures

14. The multiple nuclei model of urban structure developed by Harris and Ullman arose from the idea that _____ was losing its dominant position in the metropolitan city.
    A. the CBD
    B. the inner city
    C. public transportation
    D. the suburb
    E. private housing

15. Cities in the periphery of the world generally have which of the following?
    A. an absence of enforced zoning regulations
    B. a total lack of industry
    C. acute water shortages
    D. poor public transportation
    E. civil unrest

CHAPTER 10:
DEVELOPMENT

The Five Steps to Chapter Success Checklist

Step 1: Read the Chapter Summary below, preview the Key Questions, the Chapter Outline, and
    the terms of the chapter.
Step 2: Complete the Pre-Reading Activity (PRA) for this chapter.
Step 3: Read the chapter and complete the guided worksheet.
Step 4: As you read the chapter, complete World Region Map Sheets for every world map.
    Go to the Student Companion Website to print out the WRMS.
Step 5: Take an AP-style Practice Quiz.

STEP 1: Chapter Summary, Key Questions, Chapter Outline and Geographic Concepts

Chapter Summary

The idea of economic development is relatively new; it implies a sense of progressively improving
a country's economic situation. The idea took hold in the wake of the Industrial Revolution.
Geographers focus on the spatial structure of the economy, assessing how that structure
influences the ability of states and regions to reach greater levels of economic development.
Geographers also recognize that economic development in a single place is based on a multitude
of factors, including the situation within the global economy, the link the place plays in
commodity chains, the efficacy of government, the presence of disease, the health and well being
of the population, the presence and amount of foreign debt, the success or failure of government
policies, and the influence of nongovernmental programs. Geographers also realize that all of
these processes are operating concurrently across scales, making a country's journey toward
economic development much more complicated than climbing a ladder.

Key Questions

Field Note: Geography, Trade, and Development	335–336
1. How is development defined and measured?	337–342
2. How does geographical situation affect development??	342–344
3. What are the barriers to and the costs of economic development?	344–358
4. How do political and economic institutions influence uneven development within states?	358–362

Chapter 10 Outline

A. How Is Development Defined and Measured?
    1. Gross National Income
    2. Development Models
B. How Does Geographical Situation Affect Development?
    1. Dependency Theory
    2. Geography and Context
C. What Are the Barriers to and the Cost of Economic Development?
    1. Barriers to Economic Development
        a. Social Conditions
        b. Foreign Debt
        c. Disease
        d. Political Corruption and Instability
    2. Costs of Economic Development
        a. Industrialization
        b. Agriculture
        c. Tourism
D. How Do Political and Economic Institutions Influence Uneven Development Within States?
    1. The Role of Governments
    2. Islands of Development
    3. Creating Growth in the Periphery of the Periphery

Geographic Concepts		
Commodity Chain	Neo-Colonialism	Vectored Diseases
Developing	Structuralist Theory	Malaria
Gross National	Dependency Theory	Export Processing Zones
Product (GNP)	Dollarization	Maquiladoras
Gross Domestic	World-Systems Theory	Special Economic Zones
Gross National	Three-Tier Structure	North American Free Trade Agreement (NAFTA)
Income (GNI)	Millennium	Desertification
Per Capita (GNI)	Development Goals	Island of Development
Formal Economy	Trafficking	Nongovernmental Organizations (NGOs)
Informal Economy	Structural	Microcredit Program
Modernization Model	Adjustment Loans	
Context	Neoliberalism	

Step 2: Pre-Reading Activity (PRA)

Name: _____ **Period** _____ **Date** _____

Chapter Title: _____

Chapter # _____ **Pgs.** _____ **to** _____

1. Write down each of the Key Questions and the number of pages for each (go back to Step 1 of your textbook for answers).

Key Question	# of Pages

2. After looking over the Key Questions, looking through the outline, and reading the chapter summary, write a few sentences about what you expect to learn in general in this chapter.

3. Preview the entire chapter and look at all the maps, tables, charts, and pictures. Read the captions. Briefly describe IN YOUR OWN WORDS five maps or charts.

pg. _____ _____
pg. _____ _____
pg. _____ _____
pg. _____ _____
pg. _____ _____

4. How many world maps are there in this chapter? _____ (Go to the Student Companion Website and print out the World Map Region Worksheets needed for this chapter.)

5. Read the Field Note introduction of the chapter and list five specific facts you learned.

_____
_____
_____
_____

_____

_____

_____

_____

_____

_____

6. Go to Step 1 and look at the Geographic Concepts. Create a list of terms you think you know and terms you need to know.

I THINK I KNOW	I NEED TO LEARN

Step 3: Chapter 10 Guided Worksheet (Created by Parisa Watson)

Name: _____ **Period** _____ **Date** _____
Directions: As you read the chapter, fill in the blanks on the guided worksheet.

FIELD NOTE—GEOGRAPHY, TRADE AND DEVELOPMENT

1. When Timbuktu's trade patterns shifted with the development of sea trade routes along the west coast of Africa, it lost its _____ position.
2. A _____ _____ is a series of links connecting the many places of production and distribution and resulting in a commodity that is then exchanged on the market.

HOW IS DEVELOPMENT DEFINED AND MEASURED?

3. To say a country is developing is to say _____ is being made in technology, production, and socioeconomic well-being.

4. The difference between GDP and GNP is _____.

5. In recent years, economists have increasingly turned to _____ _____ _____, which calculates the monetary worth of what is produced within a country plus income received from investments outside the country minus income payments to other countries around the world. It is seen as a more _____ way of measuring a country's wealth in the context of the global economy.

6. The _____ _____ is the legal economy that governments tax and monitor and is limited by nature.

7. The _____ _____ is the uncounted or illegal economy that governments do not tax and keep track of, including everything from a garden plot in a year to the black market to the illegal drug trade.

8. One way to measure social welfare is the _____ _____, a measure of the number of dependents young and _____ that each 100 employed people support. A _____ dependency ratio can result in significant economic and _____ strain.

9. _____ made the modernization model and is comprised of _____ stages: _____.

10. Another name for the modernization model is _____ of _____.

11. List some general criticisms of the model: _____ _____.

HOW DOES GEOGRAPHICAL SITUATION AFFECT DEVELOPMENT?

12. Development happens in _____: it reflects what is happening in a place as a result of forces operating concurrently at multiple scales.

13. Many development scholars argue that today the poor are experiencing _____, whereby the major world powers continue to control the economies of poorer countries, even though the poorer countries are now politically independent states.

14. A _____ _____ holds that difficult to change, large-scale economic arrangements shape what can happen in fundamental ways.

15. Structuralists have developed a major body of development theory called _____ _____, which holds that the political and economic relationships between countries and regions of the world control and limit the economic development possibilities of poorer areas.

16. Many poorer countries tie their currency to a _____ country's currency. When a country's currency is eliminated in favor of the dollar, it is known as _____. _____ is an example of a country that instituted this.

17. Wallerstein's world-systems theory consists of the _____, _____ and _____. It is applicable at scales beyond the _____. A _____ relationship can exist within a _____.

WHAT ARE THE BARRIERS TO AND THE COSTS OF ECONOMIC DEVELOPMENT?

18. International _____ and governments measure development and then create programs to help improve the conditions of humans around the world, especially the _____ of the world. One of the most widely referenced measurements is the _____ _____ _____ _____ _____. The three basic dimensions are _____.

19. List a few social condition problems in periphery countries: _____.

20. _____ happens when adults and children in poor economic status leave and are deceived into working conditions that they wouldn't choose.

21. Complicating the picture further is the _____ _____ crisis that many periphery and semiperiphery countries face. In the 1980s and 1990s, the _____ _____ and International Monetary Fund were lending significant amounts of money to peripheral and semiperipheral countries, but with _____ attached. To secure the loans, countries had to agree to implement economic or _____ reforms, such as privatizing government entities, opening the country to foreign trade, reducing _____, and encouraging foreign direct investment. These loans are known as _____ _____ loans.

22. A vectored disease is one spread by one _____ to another person. Malaria is one such disease and is spread by a _____ who serves as a host. Malaria occurs throughout the world, except in _____ latitudes and _____ and drier environments. Most malaria victims are _____ under the age _____.

23. Although not addressed in the Millennium Development goals, _____ _____ and instability can greatly impede economic development as well.

24. In places where poverty is rampant, politicians often become _____, misusing aid and exacerbating the plight of the poor. _____ is an example of such a country.

25. Economic development _____ a place. To increase productivity, whether industrial or _____, people transform the environment. _____ and _____ _____ are often polluted.

26. In their efforts to attract new industries, the _____ of many countries in the global periphery and semipheriphery have set up manufacturing export zones called _____ _____ _____, which offer favorable tax, regulatory and trade arrangements to foreign firms.

27. Two of the best known of these zones are the Mexican _____ and the _____ _____ _____ of China. The _____ zone is just across the border in Mexico and the _____ _____ _____ in China are located near major ports.

28. Many maquiladora factories hire young _____ and _____ for _____ pay and few if any benefits.

29. _____ is a trade agreement between the United States, Canada, and Mexico.

30. _____ is the expansion of desert caused by _____ through overuse of the land. In Subsaharan Africa over the last 50 years, more than _____ square miles of farming and grazing land have become desert.

HOW DO POLITICAL AND ECONOMIC INSTITUTIONS INFLUENCE UNEVEN DEVELOPMENT WITHIN STATES?

31. In our globalized world, poverty is not confined to the _____. Core countries have _____ and peoples that are markedly poorer than others.

32. The actions of _____ influence whether, how, and where the wealth is produced.

33. In Wisconsin many farmers run a highly _____ farm, while in Appalachia there is little _____.

34. In both periphery and core, governments often prioritize the creation of wealth in the seat of governmental authority: the _____ _____. The African country of _____ moved its capital along with the countries of _____ and _____. Brazil moved its capital to _____ to promote migration to the _____.

35. An island of development is _____. One of the greatest challenges is creating development opportunities outside of _____ of _____.

36. _____ are organizations not run by the government but operate independently and are usually nonprofit.

37. _____ programs usually benefit women in particular in the development of small business.

Step 4: Remember to fill out World Region Map Sheets.

Go to the Student Companion Website to print out the sheets: www.wiley.com/college/Fouberg

Step 5: Practice Quiz

1. Which of the following is **not** true regarding peripheral countries and tourism?
   A. "host" countries tend not to own or control the tourism infrastructure
   B. funds for hotel construction are often diverted from local needs
   C. the tourist industry contributes substantially to the "host" country's development
   D. local leaders may have a stake in hotel/resort revenues
   E. tourists consume large quantities of scarce commodities such as food and water

2. More than 20,000 nongovernmental organizations (NGOs) in Bangladesh constitute what can be called
    A. a parallel state
    B. colonial enclaves
    C. development islands
    D. subversive zones
    E. special economic zones (SEZs)

3. Those diseases that are spread by a host or hosts are known as
    A. endemic
    B. peripheral
    C. pandemic
    D. epidemic
    E. vectored

4. Mexico has established export processing zones with special tax, trade, and regulatory arrangements for foreign firms. These zones are referred to as
    A. maquiladoras
    B. haciendas
    C. border cities
    D. NAFTA zones
    E. free trade areas

5. Measures of high levels of development can, in part, be determined by access to railways, roads, airline connections, telephones, radio and television, and so on. These are collectively referred to as
    A. infrastructure
    B. dependency measures
    C. formal economy
    D. commodity connections
    E. media links

6. Which is NOT among the five stages of Rostow's development model?
    A. traditional
    B. takeoff
    C. high mass consumption
    D. collapse-decline
    E. drive to maturity

7. Even if the gross national income (GNI) per capita index is used to measure the well-being of a country, it will fail to show
    A. growth in secondary industries (manufacturing)
    B. the distribution of wealth
    C. growth within tertiary industries (services)
    D. growth with primary industries (mining, forestry, agriculture, fishing)
    E. change in the economy over time

8. The principal structuralist alternative to Rostow's model of economic development is known as
    A. the takeoff model
    B. the liberal model
    C. the modernization model
    D. dependency theory
    E. grass roots activism

9. The continuation of economic dependence even after political independence is referred to as
    A. precondition to takeoff
    B. modernization model
    C. postcolonialism
    D. independence movement
    E. neocolonialism

10. Which of the following is NOT one of the Millennium Development Goals?
    A. eradicate HIV/AIDS by the year 2015
    B. achieve universal primary education
    C. ensure environmental sustainability
    D. promote gender equality and empower women
    E. improve maternal health

11. Which of the following is NOT associated with core production processes?
    A. technology
    B. low-wage labor
    C. education
    D. research and development
    E. modern cities

12. Which does NOT make up a portion of Colombia's GNI?
    A. professional sports franchises
    B. tourism
    C. coffee production
    D. drug trafficking
    E. flower exports

13. A large component of survival in countries with low per capita GNI is
    A. foreign aid
    B. the sales of resources
    C. the informal economy
    D. tourism
    E. prostitution

14. Subsistence forms of agriculture in peripheral areas produce little in the way of
    A. protein
    B. grain crops
    C. root crops
    D. foodstuffs
    E. useful fibers

15. A look at the maps of Nigeria, Pakistan, and Brazil would show that when governments established new postcolonial capitals, they moved away from
    A. swamps
    B. deserts
    C. areas of ethnic discord
    D. internal regions
    E. coastal port areas

CHAPTER 11:
AGRICULTURE

The Five Steps to Chapter Success Checklist

Step 1: Read the Chapter Summary below, preview the Key Questions, the Chapter Outline, and the terms of the chapter.

Step 2: Complete the Pre-Reading Activity (PRA) for this chapter.

Step 3: Read the chapter and complete the guided worksheet.

Step 4: As you read the chapter, complete World Region Map Sheets for every world map.
Go to the Student Companion Website to print out the WRMS.

Step 5: Take an AP-style Practice Quiz.

STEP 1: Chapter Summary, Key Questions, Chapter Outline and Geographic Concepts

Chapter Summary

Agricultural production has changed drastically since the First Agricultural Revolution. Today, agricultural products, even perishable ones, are shipped around the world. Agriculture has industrialized, and in many places, food production is dominated by large-scale agribusiness. A major commonality between ancient agriculture and modern agriculture remains: the need to change. Trial and error were the norms of early plant and animal domestication. Agriculture makes distinct impressions on the cultural landscape, from how land surveys, to land ownership, to land use. In the globalized economy, what is produced where depends on many factors, from climate and government regulation to technology and worldwide demand for crops.

Key Questions

Field Note: Changing Greens	365–367
1. What is agriculture, and where did agriculture begin?	368–375
2. How did agriculture change with industrialization?	375–381
3. What imprint does agriculture make on the cultural landscape?	381–386
4. How is agriculture currently organized geographically, and how has agribusiness influenced the contemporary geography of agriculture?	386–401

Chapter 11 Outline

A. What Is Agriculture, and Where Did Agriculture Begin?
   1. Hunting, Gathering, and Fishing
   2. Terrain and Tools
   3. The First Agricultural Revolution
   4. Domestication of Animals
   5. Subsistence Agriculture
B. How Did Agriculture Change With Industrialization?
   1. Understanding the Spatial Layout of Agriculture
   2. The Third Agricultural Revolution
   3. New Genetically Modified Foods
   4. Regional and Local Change
   5. The Impact of Agricultural Modernization on Earlier Practices
C. What Imprint Does Agriculture Make on the Cultural Landscape?
   1. Villages
   2. Functional Differentiation within Villages
D. How Is Agriculture Currently Organized Geographically, and How Has Agribusiness Influenced the Contemporary Geography of Agriculture?
   1. The World of Climates
   2. The World Map of Agriculture
      a. Cash Crops and Plantations Agriculture
      b. Commercial Livestock, Fruit, and Grain Agriculture
      c. Subsistence Agriculture
      d. Mediterranean Agriculture
      e. Drug Agriculture
      f. Informal Agriculture
   3. Political Influences on Agriculture
   4. Social-cultural Influences on Agriculture
   5. Agribusiness and the Changing Geography of Agriculture
   6. Environmental Impacts of Commercial Agriculture
   7. The Challenge of Feeding Everyone

Geographic Concepts		
Organic Agriculture	Shifting Cultivation	Monoculture
Agriculture	Slash-and-Burn Agriculture	Köppen Climatic
Primary Economic Activity	Second Agricultural Revolution	Classification System
Secondary Economic Activity	Von Thünen Model	Climatic Regions
Tertiary Economic Activity	Third Agricultural Revolution	Plantation Agriculture
Quaternary Economic Activity	Green Revolution	Livestock Ranching
Quinary Economic Activity	Genetically Modified Organisms (GMOs)	Mediterranean Agriculture

Plant Domestication	Rectangular Survey System	Cash Crops
Root Crops	Township- and Range-System	Luxury Crops
Seed Crops	Metes and Bounds System	Agribusiness
First Agricultural Revolution	Long-Lot Survey System	Food Desert
Animal Domestication	Primogeniture	
Subsistence Agriculture	Commercial Agriculture	

Step 2: Pre-Reading Activity (PRA)

Name: _____ **Period** _____ **Date** _____

Chapter Title: _____

Chapter # _____   **Pgs.** _____ **to** _____

1. Write down each of the Key Questions and the number of pages for each (go back to Step 1 of your textbook for answers).

Key Question	# of Pages

2. After looking over the key questions, looking through the outline, and reading the chapter summary, write a few sentences about what you expect to learn in general in this chapter.

3. Preview the entire chapter and look at all the maps, tables, charts, and pictures. Read the captions. Briefly describe IN YOUR OWN WORDS five maps or charts.

pg. _____ _____

pg. _____ _____

pg. _____ _____

pg. _____ _____

pg. _____ _____

4.   How many world maps are there in this chapter? _____ (Go to the Student Companion
     Website and print out the World Map Region Worksheets needed for this chapter.)

5.   Read the Field Note introduction of the chapter and list five specific facts you learned.

     _____

     _____

     _____

     _____

     _____

     _____

     _____

     _____

     _____

     _____

6.   Go to Step 1 and look at the Geographic Concepts. Create a list of terms you think you know
     and terms you need to know.

I THINK I KNOW	I NEED TO LEARN

Step 3: Chapter 11 Guided Worksheet (Created by Parisa Watson)

Name: _____ **Period** _____ **Date** _____

Directions: As you read the chapter, fill in the blanks on the guided worksheet.

FIELD NOTE–CHANGING GREENS

1. Cattle ranchers in _____ _____ started growing soybeans when genetically modified _____ made it possible to grow the crop there.
2. _____ is a company that produces Roundup.
3. The production of crops without the use of pesticides and fertilizers is called _____ _____. Although they are found everywhere, most are sold in the _____ _____ _____ in countries such as the United States, Canada, Japan, Australia, and countries in Europe. Some benefits of organic agriculture include: _____.

WHAT IS AGRICULTURE, AND WHERE DID AGRICULTURE BEGIN?

4. _____ is the deliberate tending of crops and livestock to produce food, feed, fiber, and fuel.
5. Economic activities that involve the _____ of economically valuable products from the earth, including agriculture, ranching, hunting, and gathering, fishing, forestry, mining, and quarrying, are called _____ economic activities.
6. Activities that take a primary product and change it into something else such as toys, ships, processed foods, chemicals, and _____ are _____ economic activities. _____ is the principal secondary activity.
7. _____ economic activities are those service industries that connect producers to consumers and facilitate commerce and trade or help people meet their needs. List some occupations that are involved with this type of economic activity: _____.
8. Quarternary economic activities involve _____, while quinary activities involve _____.
9. Examining the proportion of people employed in a given economic sector gives us a basic idea of how the good is _____. For example, in Guatemala, _____% of the labor force is employed in agriculture. Contrast this with Canada, which only has ___% of the labor force employed in agriculture. The tertiary sector of _____ is 75%, contrasted with Guatemala's _____%.
10. The high proportion of agriculture in Guatemala tells us that there is a lack of _____. In the United States, less than _____% is employed in agriculture. In the United States, agricultural _____ is at an all-time high.
11. Before the advent of agriculture, hunting, _____, and fishing were the most common means of subsistence throughout the world. Before developing _____, hunter-

gatherers worked on perfecting tools, controlling _____, and adapting to their environmental needs. The first tools in hunting were simple _____. The use of controlled _____ was another important achievement of human communities.

12. Carl Sauer studied the geography of the _____ Agricultural Revolution, focusing on the location of agricultural hearths and what kinds of agricultural innovations took place in those hearths.

13. _____, _____, and _____ are examples of root crops.

14. The majority of people believe seed crops first developed in _____. The cultivation of seed crops marked the beginning of what has been called the _____ _____ _____. The grain crops _____ and _____ grew well in the warm Southwest Asian climate.

15. In Southeast Asia, _____, _____, and _____ were the leading food plants. In Southwest Asia, plant domestication centered on _____, _____ and other grains. In the Mesoamerican region, the basic plants were _____ (_____), _____ and several kinds of _____.

16. Some scholars believe that _____ _____ began earlier than plant domestication. It must have emerged over time, in stages. People kept animals for _____ purposes as well as for _____ and other reasons. Quite possibly, animals attached themselves to human settlements as _____. Goats were domesticated in the _____ Mountains, and sheep in _____.

17. Subsistence agriculture is growing only enough food to _____. It declined during the 1900s with the diffusion of _____ agriculture. A return to _____ _____ has taken hold in parts of the world where farmers feel production for the global market has not benefited them either _____ or culturally.

18. Some _____ _____ are sedentary, living in one place throughout the year, but many others move from place to place in search of better land. The latter engage in a form of agriculture known as _____ _____. It is found primarily in _____ and _____ zones where traditional farmers had to abandon plots of land after the soil became infertile. The regions quickly lose their _____, and farmers are forced to move to another parcel of _____. They then clear the _____, turn the _____ and _____ again.

19. One specific kind of shifting cultivation is _____ and _____ agriculture, also called _____, _____, or _____ agriculture. Trees are _____ _____, farmers _____ down trees, and all existing vegetation is _____ off. A layer of _____ then forms on the ground and contributes to the soil's fertility.

HOW DID AGRICULTURE CHANGE WITH INDUSTRIALIZATION?

20. For the _____ _____ to take root, a _____ _____ _____ had to take place. _____ are some of the main aspects of the Second Agricultural Revolution.

21. New _____ improved production as well. The _____ _____ enabled farmers to avoid wasting seeds and to plant in rows, making it simpler to distinguish weeds from crops. The Revolution is associated with the time frame of _____.

22. When commercial agriculture is geared to producing food for people who live in a nearby town or _____, a geographical pattern of land use based on the _____ of products and the cost of _____ emerges. In the 1800s, von Thünen experienced the _____ Agricultural Revolution first hand. He noted that as one moved _____ from the town, one commodity or _____ gave way to another. Nearest to the town, farmers produced commodities that were _____ and commanded high prices, such as _____ products and _____. Much effort would go into production because of the value of the _____ closer to the city. In his time, the town was still surrounded by _____ that provided wood for fuel and burning. In the next _____ further out crops were _____ perishable and bulkier, including _____ and other grains. Still further out, _____ _____ began to replace field crops.

23. The von Thünen model had certain assumptions:

    _____.

24. According to the von Thünen model, _____ costs would govern the use of the land. He reasoned that the greater the _____ to the market, the higher the _____ costs had to be added to the cost of producing a crop or commodity. The model is often described as the first effort to analyze the _____ character of economic activity.

25. Geographer Lee Liu studied the spatial pattern of agricultural production in _____. He noted that in lands closer to the village the soil was _____ and productive.

26. The _____ Agricultural Revolution is also called the Green _____ and dates back to the _____. It involves _____.

27. Americans funded research on maize in _____ and found a hybrid seed so that by 1960 the country was no longer _____ _____. In 1960 the focus shifted to _____ and mixing varieties of _____, first with IR8 and IR 36. As a result, India became _____ in grain production by the 1980s.

28. The impact of the Green Revolution is highly _____ as the traditional focus of _____, _____ and _____ means it only has limited impact in much of _____.

29. The promise of increasing _____ _____ in a world in which almost a billion people are malnourished has led many people to _____ genetically engineered foods. However, others question the _____ risks and _____ hazards. There is also growing concern that higher inputs of _____ _____, herbicides, and pesticides can lead to reduced organic matter and _____ _____.

30. An entire field of biotechnology has sprung up in conjunction with the _____ _____ _____ and the development of _____ _____ _____. GMOs involve (define) _____. They are found in ____% of processed foods in the United States. Resistance is found in some places such as western _____.

WHAT IMPRINT DOES AGRICULTURE MAKE ON THE CULTURAL LANDSCAPE?

31. The pattern of land ownership seen in the landscape reflects the _____ _____—the method of land survey through which land ownership and property lines are defined.

32. The _____ _____ _____ prevails throughout much of the United States and appears as checkerboards across agricultural fields. The U.S. government adopted the system after the American Revolution as part of a cadastral system known as _____ system. The basic unit was the _____ mile section.

33. _____ and _____ survey is found along the eastern seaboard and uses physical features to demarcate irregular lots.

34. The long-lot survey can be found in the states of _____ and involves the use of long, _____ lots.

35. Primogeniture is a Germanic system in which all land passes to the _____ _____.

36. Unlike Japan, in the U.S. Midwest individual farmhouses lie quite far apart in what we call _____ _____. _____ _____ is by far the most prevalent rural residential pattern in agricultural areas and involves groupings or tiny _____ or hamlets. The _____ village is also called _____ and is found in eastern Europe and East Africa. _____ _____ still exist in many rural areas of many countries and are reminders of a turbulent past. More modern villages are arranged on a _____ _____.

37. Villages everywhere display common qualities, including evidence of social stratification and _____ of buildings. The _____ _____ of buildings within farm villages is more elaborate in some societies than in others.

HOW IS AGRICULTURE CURRENTLY ORGANIZED GEOGRAPHICALLY, AND HOW HAS AGRIBUSINESS INFLUENCED THE CONTEMPORARY GEOGRAPHY OF AGRICULTURE?

38. _____ _____ has come to dominate in the world's economic _____, as well as some places in the _____ and _____. It involves _____ scale grain producers and cattle ranches, _____ equipment and factory-type labor forces, of plantations and profit. It began in the _____ and _____ centuries when Europe became a market for agricultural products from around the world.

39. Major changes in transportation and food storage, especially _____, further intertwined agricultural production and food processing regions around the world during the twentieth century. The _____ industry of Argentina thrived as a result.

40. _____ made the climate map on the basis of temperature and precipitation. The dry summer climates are known as _____ climates and are found in areas such as _____.

41. _____ are examples of plantation crops.

42. Dairying is mainly found in these regions (Figure 11.18):

_____

43. _____ _____ involves the raising of domesticated animals for the production of meat and byproducts such as leather and _____. In addition to the large cattle-ranching areas of the United States, Canada, and Mexico, much of eastern _____ and _____ are devoted to ranching.

44. _____ _____ appears on the map as a primarily subsistence grain-growing area.

45. Only one form of agriculture mentioned in the legend of Figure 11.18 refers to a particular climate zone: _____. Crops include: _____.

46. Because of the high demand for drugs in the global economic _____, some farmers in the _____ find it more profitable to cultivate poppy, coca, or marijuana plants than to grow standard food crops.

47. One of the most significant contemporary cash crops is _____. One of the most common ways in which governments influence agriculture is through tax regulations and _____ favoring certain land uses.

48. Agriculture is also affected by social and _____ factors. _____ is one of the most important luxury crops in the modern world. It was first domesticated in _____ but is now primarily grown in _____ and _____ America. It is now the _____ most valuable traded commodity in the world.

49. In most cases coffee is produced on enormous, _____ plantations, where it is picked by local laborers who are hired at very _____ wage rates. Recently coffee production has experienced changes as consumers demand _____ _____ coffee. If a retailer is Fair Trade certified, ____% of the retail price goes back to the growers. Fair trade pressured the chain _____ into selling their coffee. The push for it shows how _____ movements can influence agriculture.

50. _____ is a term for the businesses that provide a vast array of goods and services to support the agriculture industry. Early in the twentieth century, _____ production was highly disaggregated. Now, _____ breeding has produced faster growing, bigger chickens which are housed in enormous _____ houses that are largely _____. _____ houses are concentrated in _____.

51. Commercial agriculture creates significant _____ change. The growing demand for _____ foods and more efficient technologies are leading to _____ in many regions of the world.

52. The growth of _____ farming and the move toward the use of _____ foods in some communities can benefit the environment. In recent decades, the popularity of fast-food chains that serve hamburgers has led to the _____ of wooded areas in order to open up additional pastures for _____ cattle, notably in Central and South America.

53. Food riots in low-income countries remind us that food security remains a _____ for millions of people around the globe. Currently enough food is being _____, but there is _____ distribution system and widespread poverty. As cities expand, some of the most fertile land is lost to _____ and _____ developments.

54. As a result of the growing _____ between farmers and consumers, geographers draw attention to _____ _____, areas that have limited access to fresh, nutritious food.

Step 4: Remember to fill out World Region Map Sheets.

Go to the Student Companion Website to print out the sheets: www.wiley.com/college/ Fouberg

Step 5: Practice Quiz

Chapter 11: Agriculture

Multiple Choice Questions

1. In recent years, many wooded areas in _____ have been deforested to provide beef for hamburgers for fast-food chains in the United States.
    A.   East and South Asia
    B.   West Africa
    C.   East Africa
    D.   Central and South America
    E.   Canada

2. Rice cultivation is Southeast Asia is largely a _____ activity.
    A.   luxury
    B.   commercial
    C.   government
    D.   mechanized
    E.   subsistence

3. Twenty-five percent of world sugar production takes place in the United States, western Europe, and Russia, which is outside of the tropical plantation region and is produced from
    A.   genetically modified, cold-tolerant sugar cane
    B.   sugar beets
    C.   wood cellulose
    D.   artificial food chemical processes
    E.   corn syrup

4. Which of the following is INCORRECT with respect to broiler chicken sales in the United States in 2007?
    A.   most broilers are grown in uplands regions
    B.   broiler production is done on prime farmland
    C.   production operations are highly mechanized
    D.   broiler production is clustered in poorer regions
    E.   selective breeding has increased production

5. Coffee was domesticated in Ethiopia. Today, 70% of production is in
    A. Southeast Asia
    B. South Asia
    C. East Africa
    D. Middle and South America
    E. North America

6. Fair trade coffee buyers certify that _____ % of the retail price of their coffee goes to the coffee
    growers.
    A. 80
    B. 100
    C. 40
    D. 5
    E. 15

7. The rectangular land division scheme in the United States adopted after the American
    Revolution is quite unique. Its correct name is
    A. long-lot system
    B. metes and bounds system
    C. mile-grid system
    D. Franklin's system
    E. township-and-range system

8. According to Spencer and Thomas, each agricultural hearth was associated with a local
    grouping of plants. For example, taro, yams, and bananas are associated with the _____
    hearth.
    A. Meso-American
    B. Southeast Asian
    C. Southwest Asian
    D. Ethiopia-East African
    E. Amazonian

9. A form of tropical subsistence agriculture in which fields are rotated after short periods of
    crop production is
    A. subsistence rice cultivation
    B. subsistence wheat cultivation
    C. shifting cultivation
    D. nomadic herding
    E. slash-and-burn

10. Biogenetic engineering now allows the growing of new plant strains in more arid regions of the Plains States to meet the demand of the _____ industry.
    A. cattle feed
    B. bio-diesel fuel
    C. tofu/organic food
    D. grain export
    E. famine aid

11. Which is NOT an example of a primary economic activity?
    A. corn flake production
    B. iron ore production
    C. lobster fishing
    D. forestry
    E. petroleum extraction

12. In areas of shifting cultivation the population
    A. increases significantly
    B. cannot have a high density
    C. must be large enough to provide surplus labor
    D. never lives in permanent settlements
    E. practices an unsustainable form of agriculture

13. Colonial powers would make subsistence farmers
    A. grow cash crops only
    B. farm on plantations in addition to farming their own land
    C. grow cash crops in addition to food crops the farmer needed to survive
    D. buy commercial fertilizer at fixed prices
    E. leave the land to work in factories

14. Before the intervention of Europeans, the societies practicing subsistence farming were quite equal because
    A. populations were small
    B. the farmers did not live in villages or other settlements
    C. land was held in communal ownership
    D. money was equally divided
    E. the form of religion, animism, emphasizes egalitarianism

15. Poorer countries, producing such crops as sugar,
    A. set the market price themselves
    B. rapidly change to a different cash crop when commodity prices decline
    C. plant less in order to drive up the prices
    D. cooperate with each other to determine global prices and demand
    E. are at the mercy of the purchasing countries that set the prices

CHAPTER 12:
INDUSTRY AND SERVICES

The Five Steps to Chapter Success Checklist

Step 1: Read the Chapter Summary below, preview the Key Questions, the Chapter Outline, and the terms of the chapter.

Step 2: Complete the Pre-Reading Activity (PRA) for this chapter.

Step 3: Read the chapter and complete the guided worksheet.

Step 4: As you read the chapter, complete World Regions Map Sheets for every world map.
   Go to the Student Companion Website to print out the WRMS.

Step 5: Take an AP-style Practice Quiz.

STEP 1: Chapter Summary, Key Questions, Chapter Outline, and Geographic Concepts

Chapter Summary

The Industrial Revolution transformed the world economically, politically, and socially. Many of the places where industrialization first took hold have since become deindustrialized, both with the relocation of manufacturing plants and with the outsourcing of steps of the production process domestically and offshore. With changing economics, places change. Some now look like ghost towns, serving merely as a reminder that industrialization took place there. Others have booming economies and are thriving, having kept industry or having successfully developed a service economy. Still other places are redefining themselves. In the next chapter, we consider another lasting effect of industrialization and deindustrialization: environmental change.

Key Questions

Field Note: Branding the Backboard	403–404
1. Where did the Industrial Revolution begin, and how did it diffuse?	405–411
2. How have the character and geography of industrial production changed?	411–426
3. How have deindustrialization and the rise of service industries altered global economic activity?	426–432

Chapter 12 Outline

A. Where Did the Industrial Revolution Begin, and How Did It Diffuse?
    1. The Industrial Revolution
    2. Diffusion to Mainland Europe
    3. Diffusion beyond Europe
    4. North America
    5. Russia and Ukraine
    6. East Asia
B. How Have the Character and Geography of Industrial Production Changed?
    1. Fordist Production
        a. Agglomeration
    2. Flexible Production and Product Life Cycle
    3. The Global Division of Labor
    4. Made in America or Designed in America?
    5. Major Influences on the Contemporary Geography of Manufacturing
        a. Transportation
        b. Regulatory Circumstances
        c. Energy
    6. New Centers of Industrial Activity
        a. The Rise of East Asia
        b. The Chinese Juggernaut
        c. The Wider World
        d. Where from Here?
C. How Have Deindustrialization and the Rise of the Service Industries Altered Global Economic Activity?
    1. Geographical Dimensions of the Service Economy
        a. New Patterns of Economic Activity
    2. High-Technology Clusters
    3. Tourism Services
    4. Place Vulnerabilities in a Service Economy

Geographic Concepts		
Industrial Revolution	Commodification	Deindustrialization
Globalization	Product Life Cycle	Newly
Fordist	Global Division of Labor	Industrializing Countries
Vertical Integration	Just-In-Time Delivery	Break-of-Bulk Point
Friction of Distance	Spatial Fix	Rust Belt
Least Cost Theory	Outsourced	Sun Belt
Agglomeration	Offshore	Growth Pole
Flexible Production System	Intermodal Connections	Technopole

Step 2: Pre-Reading Activity (PRA)

Name: _____ **Period** _____ **Date** _____

Chapter Title: _____

Chapter # _____   **Pgs.** _____ **to** _____

1. Write down each of the Key Questions and the number of pages for each (go back to Step 1 of your textbook for answers).

Key Question	# of Pages

2. After looking over the Key Questions, looking through the outline, and reading the chapter summary, write a few sentences about what you expect to learn in general in this chapter.

3. Preview the entire chapter and look at all the maps, tables, charts, and pictures. Read the captions. Briefly describe IN YOUR OWN WORDS five maps or charts.

pg. _____ _____
pg. _____ _____
pg. _____ _____
pg. _____ _____
pg. _____ _____

4. How many world maps are there in this chapter? _____ (Go to the Student Companion Website and print out the World Map Region Worksheets needed for this chapter.)

5. Read the Field Note introduction of the chapter and list five specific facts you learned.

_____
_____
_____
_____

_____
_____
_____
_____
_____
_____

6.   Go to Step 1 and look at the Geographic Concepts. Create a list of terms you think you know and terms you need to know.

I THINK I KNOW	I NEED TO LEARN

Step 3: Chapter 12 Guided Worksheet (Created by Parisa Watson)

Name: _____ **Period** _____ **Date** _____
Directions: As you read the chapter, fill in the blanks on the guided worksheet.

FIELD NOTE—BRANDING THE BACKBOARD

1.   Even in places such as Macedonia, there is still the unmistakable _____ swoosh. The company headquarters is located in _____, _____, a suburb of Portland but not a single individual in _____ is directly involved in the process of putting a _____ together. It has almost _____ contracts in over _____ countries.

WHERE DID THE INDUSTRIAL REVOLUTION BEGIN, AND HOW DID IT DIFFUSE?

2. The manufacturing of goods began long before the _____ _____. The first steps did not involve a revolutionary _____ source; improved spinning wheels were powered by _____ _____, and new _____ _____ were driven by water running downslope.

3. The eighteenth century was marked by a series of _____ that brought new uses for known energy sources (_____) and new machines to improve efficiencies (_____ _____). _____ _____ is credited for improving the steam engine. In Britain, densely populated and heavily urbanized industrial regions developed near the _____ _____. The largest such region was the _____ of north-central _____.

4. The innovations from the Industrial Revolution in Great Britain eventually diffused to _____ _____.

5. Western Europe, eastern North America, western Russia and Ukraine, and East Asia are the world's _____ _____ regions. In North America, _____ was the chief fuel for industries at the time and there was never a threat of shortage in the United States. The reserves in the United States were found from _____ _____ to the northwestern _____ _____. The Soviet Union was _____ rich. Japan has limited _____ _____ and manufacturing depends upon raw materials being imported from other parts of the world. Japan's dominant industrial region and place for urbanization is the _____ _____, which contains one-third of the nation's population.

HOW HAVE THE CHARACTER AND GEOGRAPHY OF INDUSTRIAL PRODUCTION CHANGED?

6. _____ is a set of processes that are increasing interactions, deepening relationships, and heightening interdependence without regard to country borders.

7. The manufacturing _____ of the early twentieth century can be traced in part to early innovations in the production process. Perhaps the most significant of these innovations was the mass-production assembly line pioneered by _____ _____. It was so significant that the dominant mode of mass production that endured from 1945 to 1975 is known as _____. The period is marked by a surge in both _____ _____ and mass consumption.

8. Production of automobiles at Ford's River Rouge plant in Dearborn, Michigan exemplified the _____ _____ of production common during the Fordist period. Under Fordist production, _____ was a major consideration in the location of industry.

9. _____ of _____ refers to the increase in time and cost that usually comes with increased distance over which commodities must travel. If a raw material has to be shipped hundreds of miles to a _____, rather than being manufactured right next door, the friction of distance increases.

10. Alfred Marshall argued that a particular industry, whether automobile manufacturing or furniture production, _____ in an area. He called this process _____. Marshall

explained why industries would cluster, and German economic geographer _____ _____ developed a basic model explaining where industries would cluster.

11. Weber's _____ _____ _____ focused on a factory owner's desire to minimize three categories of costs. The first and most important of these categories was _____. He suggested that the site where these costs were lowest is the place where it is least expensive to bring _____ _____ to the point of production and to distribute finished products to consumers. The second cost was that of _____. The third factor in Weber's model was similar to Marshall's theory of _____. Weber described the advantages afforded by like industries _____, which he termed _____. He held that the industries can assist each other through shared _____, _____ and _____.

12. Fordist production was based on both mass production and mass _____. As the global economy became more integrated and transportation costs _____, the advantages of concentrating production in large-scale complexes _____. As a result, in the late twentieth century many enterprises began moving toward a _____, flexible production model. This refers to a set of production processes in which the components of goods are made in _____ _____ around the globe and then brought together as needed to meet customer demand.

13. The term _____ _____ _____ is used to describe this state of affairs because firms can pick and choose among a multitude of suppliers and production strategies in distant places, and then quickly shift their choices in response to adjustments in the production _____ and consumer _____.

14. Through the process of _____, goods that were not previously bought, sold, and traded gain a monetary value and are bought, sold, and traded on the market. In this process, goods start out at a high price, and over time the price drops and sometimes moves the production of the mobile tablets to _____ the price of production and compete. Changes in the production of a good over time take place as part of a _____ _____ _____.

15. The global division of labor is _____. Time–space compression has fundamentally altered the _____ _____ ___ _____. When the world was less interconnected, most goods were produced not just close to _____ _____ but close to the point of consumption. With _____ _____ this has changed. Rather than keeping a large _____ of components or products, companies keep just what they _____ for short-term production and new parts are shipped _____ as needed.

16. Advances in information technologies and _____ coupled with the global division of labor enable companies to move production from one side to another based on calculations of what David Harvey calls a _____ _____. In choosing a production site _____ is only one consideration. "_____ is neither determinate nor insignificant as a factor in production location decisions" today (Walcott 2011, 9).

17. Major global economic players, including _____ _____, Philips, Union Carbide, and Exxon, take advantage of _____ transportation costs, favorable

_____ regulations, and expanding _____ _____ to construct vast economic networks. Most multinational corporations have moved labor-intensive manufacturing, particularly assembly activities, to _____ countries where labor is _____, regulations are _____, and tax rates are _____. The manufacturing that remains in the core is usually highly _____.

18. China and other lower wage countries are major recipients of industrial work that is _____ or moved _____. This is done to offer cost savings and when it happens _____ of a country it is said to take place _____. Research and development activities tend to be concentrated in the _____.

19. Using published sources on computer machinery and component parts, three authors figured out the _____ supply chain and calculated the value added at each step in the _____ _____. Looking at Figure 12.11, describe where the basic chip design occurs through the final assembly: Basic design: _____, design of chip modifications/firmware design and coding: _____, chip fabrication: _____, chip packaging and testing: _____, warehouse: _____, iPod assembly: _____.

20. Relatively inexpensive transportation is one of the foundations on which the _____ _____ _____ rests. Efficient _____ _____ enable manufacturers to purchase raw materials from distant sources and to distribute finished products to a widely dispersed population of consumers. Since World War II the focus has been on improving _____ _____, places where two or more modes of transportation meet in order to ease the flow of goods and reduce the costs of _____.

21. The current volume of goods shipped around the globe could not be supported without the invention of the _____ _____, whereby goods are backed in containers that are picked up by special, mechanized _____ from a container ship at an intermodal connection and placed on the back of a semitrailer _____, or on a barge, or on a railroad car.

22. Most governments are part of the _____ _____ _____, which works to negotiate rules of trade among the member states. The organization promotes free _____ and dismisses the _____ system. Most regional trade agreements encourage movement of production within the region and promote trade by minimizing _____ quotes and _____ among member countries.

23. During the mid-twentieth century, the use of _____ as an energy source gave way to _____ and _____. Despite discoveries of oil and gas in the _____ _____, Europe still depends on oil shipments of petroleum. The ____ also has oil reserves but its own supplies are far too limited to meet demand. It leads the world demand and consumption not just in oil, but _____ ____ too.

24. As a result of advances in flexible production, over the last 30 years many older manufacturing regions have experienced _____, a process by which companies move industrial jobs to other regions, leaving a period of _____ unemployment and if possible, a switch to a _____ economy.

25. Throughout the better part of the twentieth century, _____ was the only global economic power in East Asia. The picture began to change with the emergence of the so-called Four Tigers of East and Southeast Asia: _____, _____, _____, and _____. These tigers developed into _____ _____ countries.

26. Hong Kong's situational advantages contributed enormously to its economic _____. The colony became mainland China's gateway to the world, a bustling port, financial center, and _____ point, where goods are transferred from one mode of transport to another. Hong Kong has been able to maintain the status of a _____ _____ _____ in China, which gives it a high degree of autonomy from mainland China.

27. China is a vast country and has a substantial _____ base. The Chinese have a high quality and quantity of _____. Industrial development was also high with a pattern of long-term _____, the existing transport network, and the location of the _____, which clustered mostly in the east of the country.

28. The northeast part of China is often referred to as the _____ _____ because of the close of many state-run _____. _____ is high and economic growth is _____. Today, the Chinese government is pushing for industrialization into the _____ of the country.

29. O'Brien and Friedman suggest that a combination of technological changes and developments in the global economy have reduced the significance of _____ and made place differences increasingly insignificant.

HOW HAVE DEINDUSTRIALIZATION AND THE RISE OF SERVICE INDUSTRIES ALTERED GLOBAL ECONOMIC ACTIVITY?

30. _____ _____ do not generate an actual, tangible product but instead encompass the range of services that are found in modern societies. _____ industries and _____ industries make up this type of economic activity. During the last three decades, both have experienced _____ _____, giving greater meaning to the term *postindustrial*.

31. The United States lost much of its industrial base with _____ manufacturing jobs moving to areas of the world with lower wages. This region of the United States, which used to be called the manufacturing belt, is now commonly called the _____ _____, evoking the image of long-abandoned, rusted-out steel factories.

32. Some secondary industrial regions have made the transition to a viable _____ economy successfully. The _____ _____ is the southern region of the United States, stretching through the Southeast and Southwest. In recent decades, _____ and financial industries have changed the economy and landscape of the area, as seen in the toponyms of stadiums.

33. Most service industries are not tied to _____ materials and do not need large amounts of energy. Major retailers not only shape the _____ of places but also change the economic prospects. _____ headquarters in Bentonville, _____ provides a striking example. If producers want to sell to the retailer, they must travel to Bentonville and

negotiate deals. To create _____ products, companies have moved production abroad and also into the state of _____.

34. Many of the call centers for technical help are located in _____ because of the _____ levels of education, vast numbers of _____ speakers, and phones routed through the _____. What matters most is _____, a workforce that is sufficiently _____ but not too expensive, and favorable _____ rates.

35. A high-technology corridor is an area designated by local or state government to benefit from _____ taxes and high-technology infrastructure, with the goal of providing high-technology jobs to the local population. California's _____ _____ is a well-known example of this concept. Once some high-technology businesses locate, others are also drawn. This is known as a _____ _____ because the concentration of these businesses spurred economic development in the surrounding area.

36. A _____ is an area planned for high technology where agglomeration built on synergy among technological companies occurs. These areas can be found in a number of countries in western Europe, _____ _____, North America, and Australia. _____ are on the scale of Silicon Valley.

37. Mechanization can also have a negative impact. In recent decades jobs have been lost in the _____ planning industry along with fewer workers at _____ because of scanners.

Step 4: Remember to fill out World Region Map Sheets.

Go to the Student Companion Website to print out the sheets: www.wiley.com/college/Fouberg

Step 5: Practice Quiz

Chapter 12: Industry and Service

Multiple Choice Questions

1. Over 50% of the goods entering Europe come through two ports in
   A. Luxembourg
   B. Belgium
   C. Netherlands
   D. Germany
   E. France

2.   Shenyang is to China as _____ was to the United States in the production of _____.
   A.   Pittsburgh; steel
   B.   Boston; textiles
   C.   Philadelphia; cheese
   D.   Hartford; insurance
   E.   Newark; shipping

3.   Service industries are commonly referred to as _____ industries.
   A.   primary
   B.   secondary
   C.   tertiary
   D.   quaternary
   E.   quinary

4.   Russia's "Detroit" southeast of Moscow is:
   A.   Kiev
   B.   St. Petersburg
   C.   Volgograd
   D.   Rostov
   E.   Nizhni Novgorod

5.   Japan's dominant industrial region is
   A.   Kitakyushu
   B.   Toyama
   C.   Kanto Plain
   D.   Kansai
   E.   Shikoku

6.   Fast, flexible production of small lots of products with outsourcing around the world is referred to as
   A.   Fordist
   B.   post-Fordist
   C.   socialist
   D.   colonial production
   E.   just-in-time

7.   Europe's greatest industrial complex is
   A.   Donbas
   B.   British Midlands
   C.   Silesia
   D.   Berlin
   E.   the Ruhr

8. The increase in time and cost with distance is referred to as
    A. production costs
    B. distribution costs
    C. friction of distance
    D. distance decay
    E. frustration

9. When Alfred Weber published his book *Theory of the Location of Industries* (1909), what did he select as the critical determinant of regional industrial location?
    A. availability of labor
    B. nearby markets
    C. costs of labor
    D. transportation costs
    E. political influence

10. The type of manufacturing that is more likely to be located in peripheral countries is
    A. technical design
    B. labor-intensive
    C. low-labor needs
    D. high-tech
    E. low value-added

11. The most important locational factor for the service sector is
    A. energy
    B. transportation
    C. market
    D. labor
    E. climate

12. Technopoles, a collection of high-technology industries, can be found in a number of countries. Which of the following is NOT a region containing one of these countries?
    A. eastern Asia
    B. India
    C. Australia
    D. North America
    E. Africa

CHAPTER 13:
THE HUMANIZED ENVIRONMENT

The Five Steps to Chapter Success Checklist

Step 1: Read the Chapter Summary below, preview the Key Questions, the Chapter Outline, and the terms of the chapter.

Step 2: Complete the Pre-Reading Activity (PRA) for this chapter.

Step 3: Read the chapter and complete the guided worksheet.

Step 4: As you read the chapter, complete World Region Map Sheets for every world map.
Go to the Student Companion Website to print out the WRMS.

Step 5: Take an AP-style Practice Quiz.

STEP 1: Chapter Summary, Key Questions, Chapter Outline, and Geographic Concepts

Chapter Summary

What will the future be like? Many would agree with geographer Robert Kates, who foresees a "warmer, more crowded, more connected but more diverse world." As we consider this prospect, we must acknowledge that global environmental changes illustrate the limits of what we know about our planet. Global environmental change is not always anticipated and is often nonlinear. Some changes are "chaotic" in the sense that future conditions cannot be reliably predicted. Nonlinearity means that small actions in certain situations may result in large impacts and may be more important than larger actions in causing change. Thresholds also exist in many systems, which, once past, are irreversible. Irreversible changes occur, for example, when the habitat for a species is diminished to the point where the species quickly dies off. Unfortunately, we may not be able to identify these thresholds until we pass them. This leaves open the possibility of "surprises"—unanticipated responses by physical systems.

The complexity and urgency of the environmental challenge will tax the energies of the scientific and policy communities for some time to come. Geography must be an essential part of any serious effort to grapple with these challenges. The major changes that are taking place have different origins and spatial expressions, and each results from a unique combination of physical and social processes. We cannot simply focus on system dynamics and generalized causal relationships. We must also consider emerging patterns of environmental change and the impacts of differences from place to place on the operation of general processes. Geography is not the backdrop to the changes taking place; it is at the very heart of the changes themselves.

Key Questions

Field Note: Disaster along Indian Ocean Shores	434–436
1. How has Earth's environment changed over time?	437–443
2. How have humans altered Earth's environment?	443–452
3. What are the major factors contributing to environmental change today?	452–459
4. What policies are being adopted in response to environmental change?	459–462

Chapter 13 Outline

A.   How Has Earth's Environment Changed Over Time?
    1.   Tectonic Plates
    2.   Ocean and Atmosphere
    3.   Fire and Ice
    4.   The Little Ice Age in the Modern Era

B.   How Have Humans Altered Earth's Environment?
    1.   Water
        a.   Water Security
        b.   Water and Politics in the Middle East
    2.   Atmosphere
        a.   Extreme Weather Events
        b.   Acid Rain
    3.   The Land
        a.   Soil Erosion
        b.   Waste Disposal
    4.   Biodiversity

C.   What Are the Major Factors Contributing to Environmental Change Today?
    1.   Political Ecology
    2.   Population
    3.   Patterns of Consumption
    4.   Industrial Technology
    5.   Transportation
    6.   Energy
        a.   Alternative Energy

D.   What Policies Are Being Adopted in Response to Environmental Change?
    1.   Biological Diversity
    2.   Protection of the Ozone Layer
    3.   Global Climate Change

Geographic Concepts		
Chlorofluorocarbons	Holocene	Soil Erosion
Anthropocene	Little Ice Age	Solid Waste
Pangaea	Greenhouse Effect	Sanitary Landfills
Tectonic Plates	Environmental Stress	Toxic Waste
Photosynthesis	Renewable Resources	Radioactive Waste
Mass Depletions	Nonrenewable Resources	Biodiversity
Mass Extinctions	Aquifers	Rare Earth Elements
Pacific Ring of Fire	Hydrologic Cycle	Ozone Layer
Pleistocene	Atmosphere	Vienna Convention for the
Glaciation	Acid Rain	Protection of the Ozone
Interglacials	Oxygen Cycle	Layer
Wisonconsinian Glaciation	Deforestation	Montreal Protocol

Step 2: Pre-Reading Activity (PRA)

Name: _____ **Period** _____ **Date** _____

Chapter Title: _____

Chapter # _____   **Pgs.** _____ **to** _____

1. Write down each of the Key Questions and the number of pages for each (go back to Step 1 of your textbook for answers).

Key Question	# of Pages

2. After looking over the Key Questions, looking through the outline, and reading the chapter summary, write a few sentences about what you expect to learn in general in this chapter.

3.   Preview the entire chapter and look at all the maps, tables, charts, and pictures. Read the captions. Briefly describe IN YOUR OWN WORDS five maps or charts.

pg. _____ _____

pg. _____ _____

pg. _____ _____

pg. _____ _____

pg. _____ _____

4.   How many world maps are there in this chapter? _____ (Go to the Student Companion Website and print out the World Map Region Worksheets needed for this chapter.)

5.   Read the Field Note introduction of the chapter and list five specific facts you learned.

_____

_____

_____

_____

_____

_____

_____

_____

_____

_____

_____

6.   Go to Step 1 and look at the Geographic Concepts. Create a list of terms you think you know and terms you need to know.

I THINK I KNOW	I NEED TO LEARN

Step 3: Chapter 13 Guided Worksheet (Created by Parisa Watson)

Name: _____ **Period** _____ **Date** _____
Directions: As you read the chapter, fill in the blanks on the guided worksheet.

FIELD NOTE—DISASTER ALONG INDIAN OCEAN SHORELINES

1. On December 26, 2004 a tsunami struck the country of ____ _____. A tsunami results
    from an undersea _____ involving a large displacement of the Earth's crust. If you
    were on a cruise ship in the ocean during a tsunami, your boat would simply be _____ up
    and lowered. When a tsunami reaches a beach, it breaks with waves over ____ feet high. The
    Japanese tsunami in 2011 reminds us that the hazard is _____.
2. The release of _____ contributes to the growing hole in the ozone centered over
    Antarctica.

HOW HAS EARTH'S ENVIRONMENT CHANGED OVER TIME?

3. Environmental variation, spatial as well as temporal, is one of _____ crucial characteristics.
    Modern ____ _____ emerged less than 200,000 years ago and have altered the
    _____ ever since.
4. During our brief presence on the planet, humans have had a powerful impact on
    environments ranging from _____ to _____. The size of our population, our
    rapid escalation in _____, magnifies humanity's impact on Earth in unprecedented
    ways. This gave way to what Paul Crutzen defined as the newest geologic epoch called the
    _____ to acknowledge the incredible role humans play in shaping Earth's
    environment.
5. Climatologist Alfred _____ used his spatial view of the world to make a key contribution.
    His continental drift hypothesis required the preexistence of a supercontinent, which he
    called _____, that broke apart into the fragments we now know as Africa, the
    Americas, Eurasia, and Australia. The latest breakup began _____ million years ago and
    continues to this day.
6. Earth is often called the Blue Planet because more than ____ % of its surface is covered by
    water. We don't exactly know how the Earth got its water, nor do we know how the
    _____ was formed. _____ is the conversion of carbon dioxide and
    water into carbohydrates and oxygen through the absorption of sunlight.
7. Episodes of incalculable volumes of gas and ash into the atmosphere caused _____ _____
    (_____ of diversity) and contributed to _____ _____ (mass destruction of most
    species) known to have occurred over the past 500 million years.
8. The _____ _____ ____ _____ is an area of the ocean/world that experiences frequent
    earthquakes and volcanoes. During the _____ epoch which opened less than 2 million
    years ago, the planet was in a deep freeze. The epoch was marked by long _____
    and short, warm _____.

9.   The _____ _____ is the most recent glaciations of the Pleistocene.
10. Mount Toba erupted _____ years ago, sending millions of debris into orbit, obscuring the sun, creating long-term darkness, and altering global _____.
11. _____ is the interglaciation found today.
12. Famines struck all over Europe. The climatic record was pieced together from farmers' _____ (_____ _____ were especially useful). The cooling period was named the _____ _____ _____ rather than Minor Glaciation. It helps explain why Jamestown _____ so fast. Tree ring studies found that Jamestown experienced a seven-year _____. As it continued into the 1800s, a large-scale _____ had a major impact on society. It was the the Tambora Volcano on the island of _____.

HOW HAVE HUMANS ALTERED EARTH'S ENVIRONMENT?

13. Biologists estimate that as many as _____ million types of organisms inhabit the Earth, perhaps even more. No species ever affected the environment as much as _____ do today. It is even suggested that the next great _____ will be caused by _____ and not asteroids.
14. Some obvious environmental stress is more obvious because it takes place around humans, such as _____ forests, _____ pollutants into the atmosphere. Less obvious examples include burying _____ waste and dumping _____ into the ocean.
15. Water is an example of a _____ resource, resources that are replenished as they are being used. Resources that are present in finite quantities are _____ _____.
16. _____ are water-holding rocks that provide millions of wells with steady flows. It is estimated that in the United States alone there are _____ times as much water stored there. Floridians overuse the _____ _____, and saltwater enters it from the Atlantic Ocean, which could lead to permanently _____ a fresh water aquifer.
17. One of the greatest ecological disasters of the twentieth century occurred in _____ and _____, whose common boundary runs through the Aral Sea. Streams that fed the sea were diverted to _____ the surrounding desert. Eventually the Aral Sea began to _____ up and has lost more than _____ of its total surface area.
18. The hydrologic cycle involves water from the oceans, lakes, soil, rivers, and vegetation _____, condenses, and then precipitates on landmasses. It does not take into account _____ regions of the world, and also assumes water cycles in predictable way.
19. Water supply is a particularly difficult problem affecting relations among _____ and its neighbors. As much as _____ of Israel's water comes from sources outside of the state. Key sources of water are the _____ river and an aquifer beneath the _____ _____. The _____ issue will complicate any hoped-for settlement of territorial disputes among Israel and its neighbors.
20. The _____ is a thin layer of air lying directly above the lands and oceans. We depend on it for _____.

21. The amounts of key "_____" gases, carbon dioxide, methane and nitrous oxides in the atmosphere have been increasing at a rate of about 2% per decade. _____, steel mills, refineries, and chemical plants account for a part of this increase. While estimates of the degree of human-induced _____ _____ differ, climate records from recent decades show that global temperatures are rising.

22. Acid rain forms when _____ _____ and _____ _____ are released into the atmosphere by the burning of fossil fuels. Acid rain is found in the regions of

_____.

23. Forests cover _____% of the total surface of the Earth. They play a critical role in the

_____ _____.

24. _____ occurs when forests are cut for agricultural production, wood, and paper products. In the early 1980s a study came out showing that _____% of tropical rain forests had already been affected by cutting.

25. A few reasons why soil erosion has increased involves humans cultivating on _____ slopes or without any _____ at all.

26. The _____ is the largest producer of solid waste. According to current estimates, the United States produces _____ kilograms or _____ pounds of solid waste per person per day.

27. Disposal of these wastes is a _____ problem. In poorer countries waste is often thrown onto _____ dumps. In countries that can afford it, these have been replaced by _____ _____ where a floor of materials to treat seeking liquids has been prepared.

28. _____ _____ is caused by chemicals and other infectious materials such as radioactive waste, which are of two types: low-level wastes, which give off _____ level amounts of radiation and are produced by hospitals and nuclear power plants; and _____ radioactive wastes, which emit strong radiation and are produced by nuclear power plants and nuclear weapons factories. The latter are extremely dangerous and difficult to _____ _____ of.

29. A significant change that is related to all of the developments discussed so far is the accelerating loss of _____. It refers to the varieties of species found on Earth. Human impacts on biodiversity have _____ over time. Many birds and _____ have been hunted for their food and feathers, skins, and furs. Worldwide, elephants and _____ continue to be hunted for ivory tusks.

30. Humans have also indirectly contributed to _____. A famous example is the _____ bird. An estimated _____ species of birds on tropical Pacific Islands became extinct following human settlement.

WHAT ARE THE MAJOR FACTORS CONTRIBUTING TO ENVIRONMENTAL CHANGE TODAY?

31. _____ _____ use scale to consider how attempts to affect environmental change, such as deforestation, differ depending on the level of spatial detail used to examine the issue.

Mosley studied farmers in Mali and discovered that they were more likely to use _____ materials to preserve topsoil and that wealthier farmers were more likely to use _____ fertilizers and pesticides.

32. _____ affect the environment, and a greater number of people on Earth translates into a _____ capacity for environmental change.

33. It has been estimated that a baby born in the United States during the first decade of the twenty-first century consumes about _____ times as much energy over a lifetime than a baby born in _____.

34. The demand for low-cost _____ for hamburgers in the United States has led to _____ in Central and South America to make way for pastures and cattle herds.

35. Resource extraction practices such as _____ and _____, which provide the materials to produce technologies, have created severe _____ problems.

36. Advances in _____ have produced significant pollution.

37. Concern over the long-term implications in the decline in oil revenue in Kuwait has led to efforts to find an alternative source of wealth: _____ _____.

WHAT POLICIES ARE BEING ADOPTED IN RESPONSE TO ENVIRONMENTAL CHANGE?

38. The extent and rapidity of recent environmental changes have led to the adoption of numerous policies aimed at protecting the _____ or reversing the negative impacts of _____. A major challenge in confronting environmental problems is that many of those problems do not lie within a _____ _____.

39. International concern over the loss of species led to calls for a _____ _____ as early as 1981.

40. The _____ _____ exists in the upper levels of the stratosphere and helps protect the Earth from the sun's ultraviolet rays. Studies revealed that the main culprits of CFCs were refrigerants found in fire extinguishers and aerosol cans. CFCs had only been in use since the _____.

41. International cooperation began in 1985 with the negotiation of the Vienna Convention for the Protection of the _____ _____. Specific targets and timetables for the phase-out of production and consumption of _____ were defined and agreed upon as part of the international agreement known as the _____ _____.

42. Beginning in the late 1980s, growing concern about _____ _____ led to a series of intergovernmental conferences. The _____ agreement was aimed at countries such as the United States, Japan, and the countries of the European Union to cut their greenhouse gas emissions. Neither the _____ nor _____ signed the agreement.

Step 4: Remember to fill out World Region Map Sheets.

Go to the Student Companion Website to print out the sheets: www.wiley.com/college/Fouberg

Step 5: Practice Quiz

Chapter 13: Human Environment

Multiple Choice Questions

1. The Global Environment Facility funds projects related to four issues. Which of the following is not one of these?
   A. loss of biodiversity
   B. climatic change
   C. soil erosion
   D. depletion of the ozone layer
   E. protection of international waters

2. In the early 1980s the Food and Agriculture Organization of the United Nations undertook a study of the rate of depletion of tropical rain forests and determined that _____ % had already been affected by cutting.
   A. 24
   B. 34
   C. 44
   D. 54
   E. 64

3. The United States is the most prolific producer of solid waste. Studies estimate that the United States produces about _____ pounds of solid waste per person per day.
   A. 1.5
   B. 4.5
   C. 5.5
   D. 7.3
   E. 8.1

4. The highest densities of coal and oil burning, which causes acid rain, are associated with large concentrations of heavy manufacturing such as those in
   A. southern Africa
   B. coastal South America and Asia
   C. eastern Europe and East Asia
   D. the Southern Hemisphere
   E. western and eastern Europe and the United States

5. The world distribution of precipitation is concentrated in
    A. equatorial and tropical areas
    B. mid-latitude regions
    C. high latitudes
    D. subtropical regions
    E. elevations above 5,000 feet

6. The climatic record documenting the beginning of the Little Ice Age was partially pieced together by using farmer's diaries. Those of _____ were most useful.
    A. dairy farmers
    B. Catholic monks
    C. grain farmers
    D. vegetable growers
    E. wine growers

7. Climatologist-geographer Alfred Wegener used his spatial view of the world to develop the theory of
    A. relativity
    B. the hydrologic cycle
    C. continental drift
    D. earth rotation
    E. plate subduction

8. The boundaries of crustal plates (theory of plate tectonics) are associated with
    A. deserts
    B. earthquakes and volcanoes
    C. ice caps
    D. Plains regions
    E. mountain building

9. Plant life and photosynthesis began about 1.5 billion years ago and increased the _____ level in the atmosphere.
    A. CO_2
    B. nitrogen
    C. methane
    D. sulfur
    E. O_2

10. Fifty times as much as water is stored in _____ in the United States as falls as precipitation each year.
    A. reservoirs
    B. aquifers
    C. streams
    D. lakes
    E. glaciers

11. One of the great ecological disasters of the twentieth century occurred in Uzbekistan and Kazakhstan and involves
    A. the Black Sea
    B. Lake Baikal
    C. the Aral Sea
    D. the Caspian Sea
    E. Lake Balqash

12. Forests affect the atmosphere through their role in
    A. global warming
    B. the production of CO_2
    C. desertification
    D. the oxygen cycle
    E. decomposition

CHAPTER 14:
GLOBALIZATION AND THE GEOGRAPHY OF NETWORKS

The Five Steps to Chapter Success Checklist

Step 1: Read the Chapter Summary below, preview the Key Questions, the Chapter Outline, and the terms of the chapter.

Step 2: Complete the Pre-Reading Activity (PRA) for this chapter.

Step 3: Read the chapter and complete the guided worksheet.

Step 4: As you read the chapter, complete World Region Map Sheets for every world map. Go to the Student Companion Website to print out the WRMS.

Step 5: Take an AP-style Practice Quiz.

STEP 1: Chapter Summary, Key Questions, Chapter Outline, and Geographic Concepts

Chapter Summary

Globalization has been compared to a runaway train blowing through stations, leaving much of the world to stare at its caboose. Yet this description is not entirely accurate. Globalization is a series of processes, not all of which are headed in the same direction. Even those processes headed down the globalization track are often stopped, sent back to the previous station, or derailed. The globalization track is not inevitable or irreversible (in the words of O'Loughlin, Staeheli, and Greenberg). Many of the most important globalization processes take place within networks of global cities (see Chapter 9), of places linked by popular culture (see Chapter 4), of governments (see Chapter 8), of trade (see Chapter 12), and of development (see Chapter 10). People and places are found all along these networks, and just as globalization influences people and places, those same people and places influence globalization's trajectory and future.

Key Questions

Field Note: Happiness Is in the Eye of the Beholder	464–465
How have identities changed in a globalized world?	466–469
What is globalization, and what role do networks play in globalization?	470–474
How do networks operate in a globalized world?	474–478

Chapter 14 Outline

A.   How Have Identities Changed in a Globalized World?
    1.   Personal Connectedness

B.   What Is Globalization, and What Role Do Networks Play in Globalization?
  1.   Networks
  2.   Time-Space Compression
    a.   Global Cities
C.   How Do Networks Operate in a Globalized World?
  1.   Networks with a Special Focus
    a.   Participatory Development
  2.   Networks and Information
    a.   Blogs
  3.   Networks and Economic Exchange
    a.   Community-Supported Agriculture

Geographic Concepts		
Globalization	Social Networks	Gatekeepers
Washington Consensus	Participatory Development	Horizontal Integration
Networks	Vertical Integration	Community-Supported
Digital Divide	Synergy	Agriculture

Step 2: Pre-Reading Activity (PRA)

Name: _____ **Period** _____ **Date** _____

Chapter Title: _____

Chapter # _____   **Pgs.** _____ **to** _____

1.   Write down each of the Key Questions and the number of pages for each (go back to Step 1 of your textbook for answers).

Key Question	# of Pages

2.   After looking over the Key Questions, looking through the outline and reading the chapter
     summary, write a few sentences about what you expect to learn in general in this chapter.

3.   Preview the entire chapter and look at all the maps, tables, charts, and pictures. Read the
     captions. Briefly describe IN YOUR OWN WORDS five maps or charts.

pg. _____ _____

pg. _____ _____

pg. _____ _____

pg. _____ _____

pg. _____ _____

4.   How many world maps are there in this chapter? _____ (Go to the Student Companion
     Website and print out the World Map Region Worksheets needed for this chapter.)

5.   Read the Field Note introduction of the chapter and list five specific facts you learned.

     _____

     _____

     _____

     _____

     _____

     _____

     _____

     _____

     _____

     _____

     _____

6.   Go to Step 1 and look at the Geographic Concepts. Create a list of terms you think you know
     and terms you need to know.

I THINK I KNOW	I NEED TO LEARN

Step 3: Chapter 14 Guided Worksheet (Created by Parisa Watson)

Name: _____ **Period** _____ **Date** _____

Directions: As you read the chapter, fill in the blanks on the guided worksheet.

FIELD NOTE—HAPPINESS IS IN THE EYE OF THE BEHOLDER

1. Each of us can attest that the world is anything but _____. Each place is an imprint of _____ and has its own _____, which makes it unique. Bhutan decided to measure the wealth of a country through gross national _____.

HOW HAVE IDENTITIES CHANGED IN A GLOBALIZED WORLD?

2. At each scale we have different _____. Globalization networks link us with other people and _____. In the 1990s psychologists predicted people would have _____ social skills because of the lack of personal or face-to-face interaction in the digital age.

WHAT IS GLOBALIZATION, AND WHAT ROLE DO NETWORKS PLAY IN GLOBALIZATION?

3. Globalization is a set of processes that are increasing _____, deepening relationships, and heightening interdependence without regard to _____. The backbone of globalization is _____.

4. Opponents see the Washington Consensus as a _____ push for the rest of the world.

5. _____ are a set of interconnected nodes without a center.

6. Access to information technology networks creates _____ _____. Certain places such as global cities are _____ connected than ever through communication and transportation.

7. A major divide in the access to information technology is called the _____ _____. In 2010 it was reported that average developed states had _____ telephone connections, _____ cellular connections, and _____ Internet users for every 100 people. On average, developing states had _____ telephone connections, _____ cellular connections, and _____ Internet users for every 100 people.

8.   Time–space compression has helped to create and reinforce a network of highly linked _____ _____.

HOW DO NETWORKS OPERATE IN A GLOBALIZED WORLD?

9.   The term _____ defines any number of interlinkages across the globe, whether transportation, educational, financial, or social.

10. In the spring awakening in 2011, Egyptians rose up to protest government repression by President Hosni _____, who had ruled the country for ____ years.

11. Protests rose around North Africa and Southwest Asia, from Tunisia to Yemen and _____ to _____ and to Libya. Social networks, especially _____ and _____, were credited with making revolutions in Tunisia and Egypt possible.

12. _____ _____ are nonprofit institutions outside of formal governance structures that are established to promote particular social or humanitarian ends. Each is a social network, where people with like _____ communicate to achieve a goal. This serves as a counterbalance to the power of the major _____ makers in the world. Many of their goals are to include the voices of the _____ and those directly affected by development.

13. Participatory development—the idea that _____ should be engaged in deciding what development means for them and how to achieve it—is another response to top-down decision making. The program has _____ for many farmers, though not the _____.

14. The global division of products and ideas associated with _____ culture depends largely on globalized media and retail store networks, as well as the advertising practices in which both engage. Media corporations such as Disney and Time-Warner are masters of _____ _____. It also helps media giants attract through _____, or the cross promotion of vertically integrated goods.

15. _____ are people who control access to information. Historically, governments and journalists had the ability to be strong gatekeepers by choosing what _____ to release or tell. Today with the growth of _____ on the Internet, tight gatekeeping is much more difficult.

16. Unlike major media corporations that are vertically integrated—with ownership of relevant suppliers and producers—major retail corporations are typically _____ _____. This type of corporation acquires ownership of other corporations engaged in _____ activities. It means when you shop for similar products in _____ places or across a mall, your dollars often support the same parent corporation. Banana Republic, _____ _____, and the Gap are all owned by the same _____ company.

17. One of the reasons that the number of farmers in the United States has increased is the growth of _____ _____ groups, known as CSAs. They typically use _____ growing standards but do not take the time to certify their land and produce as _____.

Step 4: Remember to fill out World Region Map Sheets.

Go to the Student Companion Website to print out the sheets: www.wiley.com/college/ Fouberg

Step 5: Practice Quiz

Chapter 14: Globalization and the Geography of Networks

Multiple Choice Questions

1. According to Manuel Castells, a set of interconnected nodes is a
    A. transport system
    B. circulation manifold
    C. network
    D. communication nexus
    E. synergy

2. The study of global cities showed that _____ is the most globally linked city in the world.
    A. New York
    B. Tokyo
    C. London
    D. Chicago
    E. Miami

3. More than anything else, globalization is driven by
    A. cultural convergence of media
    B. resource scarcities
    C. population growth
    D. trade
    E. popular culture

4. The idea that locals should be engaged in deciding what development means for them and how to achieve it is known as
    A. synergy
    B. structuralism
    C. international division of labor
    D. social networks
    E. participatory development

5.   When one company, for example, an auto parts supplier, buys several similar companies, you have an example of
     A.   horizontal integration
     B.   vertical integration
     C.   a commodity chain
     D.   globalization
     E.   diseconomies of scale

6.   The phenomenon in which two or more discrete influences or agents acting together create many more benefits together then by acting alone is known as
     A.   synergy
     B.   symbiosis
     C.   integration
     D.   gatekeeping
     E.   networking

7.   Media corporations that integrate ownership in a variety of points along the production and consumption chain are examples of
     A.   vertical integration
     B.   television networks
     C.   longitudinal cooperation
     D.   monopolies
     E.   diversification

8.   Media's power as information gatekeepers has been undercut by
     A.   local television stations and newspapers
     B.   social networks and blogs
     C.   a decline in newspaper subscription
     D.   growth in functional illiteracy
     E.   self-censure because of FCC threats about indecency

9.   The government of China works with foreign Internet companies to limit domestic access to foreign web sites that the government finds threatening—a form of censure is which search engine companies like Google comply. In this role, the government of China is the ultimate
     A.   dictator
     B.   guardian of morality
     C.   agent of change
     D.   representative of the will of people
     E.   gatekeeper

10. Many antiglobalizationists are opposed to all of the following EXCEPT
    A. increasing government-supported public services
    B. privatization of state-owned entities
    C. the opening of financial markets
    D. liberalization of trade
    E. the encouragement of direct foreign investment

PART 3: GETTING READY
FOR THE AP EXAM

Introduction: *This review section is in three parts.*

Section 1 will discuss the type of multiple choice questions you can expect on the exam with some strategies to prepare for those questions.

Section 2 focuses on the Free Response Questions (FRQs). The section will discuss the typed of Free Response Questions will appear on the AP exam and strategies to prepare you for success.

Section 3 includes two full AP-style practice exams. There are questions in the following exam which are not covered in the Fouberg, Murphy, de Blij textbook. Similarly, there are items on the APHG Exam which will not be in the textbook that you used. Therefore, it is important to go outside your text to research some of the items you might not be familiar with on the following exam.

SECTION 1
REVIEWING MULTIPLE CHOICE QUESTIONS

Remember, an AP Human Geography exam is 75 Multiple Choice Questions in 60 minutes followed by three Free Response Questions in 75 minutes. It can be overwhelming the first time a student takes it, but here are some approaches to the exam:

---

75 Multiple Choice Questions (MCQ)—The Shotgun Approach

The purpose of the MCQ portion of the exam is to assess the **breadth** of a student's geographic knowledge. The MCQs, therefore, will assess concepts, terms, models, and theories listed in the APHG Course Outline and information from every chapter in the textbooks. In other words, the "shotgun approach" means the test makers are trying to "spray" around as much geographic information as possible (much like a shotgun pattern appears on a target). So, be ready for questions from all parts of the course on the MCQs.

Three Free Response Questions (FRQ)—The Dragnet Approach

FRQs on the APHG exam should be answered using the *Dragnet Approach*, or, *Just the Facts, Ma'am*. More specifics on this are given in Section II. You are probably too young to have ever watched Sergeant Joe Friday from the old *Dragnet* TV show. His mantra was that he only wanted the facts when talking to witnesses to a crime. On the APHG FRQ section of the exam, make sure you stick to what the question is asking when answering. Unlike other AP exams, you do NOT have to write thesis statements or use any other writing style in your answers. Just answer using geographic content—or, "Just the geographic facts, ma'am!"

So, let's review the types of Multiple Choice Questions you will get on the exam.

Multiple Choice Questions

On the AP exam, there are five choices on every Multiple Choice Question. Most teachers will have four or five choice questions on their tests throughout the year. However, the type of Multiple Choice Questions may differ in difficulty based on how the question is asked. Some Multiple Choice Questions are designed for simple recall of facts; others ask you to analyze a statement; and some others might ask you to interpret a map, chart, or other data. We have included a series of types of Multiple Choice Questions you could have in class throughout the year.

1. *Recall*: These are fact-based questions that require students to recollect specific information.

People who practice slash and burn agriculture make their living as:

A.   subsistence farmers

B.   nomadic herders

C.   hunters and gatherers

D.   guest workers

E.   stateless migrants

---

2. *Determining Cause*: The word "because" is always part of the stem in this category of question. The student is expected to identify a reason for something.

Supranational organizations have become a contemporary reality largely because:

A.   the collapse of the Soviet Union and the end of the Cold War have increased polarization among nation-states

B.   of the role that globalization has played in economic and political landscape

C.   states must act unilaterally if they are to achieve their goals

D.   states in the developed realm need a power base to check the ambitions of states in the developing realm

E.   a world government is essential if there is to be international peace

---

3. *Except Questions*: AP Multiple Choice Questions are never framed using negatives. Rather the stem contains an "except" as a way of having students discriminate among possible responses.

All of the following have typically been true of plantation agriculture in Middle America except:

A.   it produces crops for export

B.   it is an inefficient operation

C.   it produces only a single crop

D.   the capital and skills necessary to support it are imported

E.   labor on the plantations is seasonal

---

4. ***Effects***: This is a modification of the recall-type question except that the student is challenged to identify *why* some phenomenon occurs.

In human geography, the process of expansion diffusion involves:
A. the spread of some innovation by a migrating people
B. the development of culture hearths in different places at different times
C. the use of innovation waves in controlling the movement of refugees
D. an innovation wave meeting with an absorbing barrier
E. the movement of a new idea or technology through an established or fixed population

5. ***True/False***: From a series of statements or phrases, the student selects the one that is accurate. Very often these are just variations of the recall-type inquiries because they expect students to identify information they have memorized.

Which of the following statements accurately describes MacKinder's heartland theory?
A. it proposed land-based power rather than ocean dominance as the determining factor in ruling the world
B. it established that a multipolar world will ensure shared power among nations
C. it hypothesized that because centripetal forces seldom counterbalance centrifugal forces, conflict within the international community is a constant reality
D. it concluded that a pivot area in the center of a landmass will always be the key factor in making a nation globally dominant
E. it argued that regardless of a state's location, power would always be determined by the abundance of its natural resources

6. ***Analyzing a Statement***: This type of question is a test of reading skills. The student is given a statement several sentences in length and asked to interpret it.

National flags within a region often share common designs but differ in colors and scales. They also reflect cultural values. The flags of Scandinavia are a good example. What is the symbol found on the flags of these countries that is a mark of their cultural identity?
A. a five-pointed star
B. a two-edged sword
C. a Latin cross
D. a gold crescent
E. a darkened oval

7. ***Interpreting Maps and Other Graphics***: Students are provided with a visual prompt that they must analyze and then identify the correct answer.

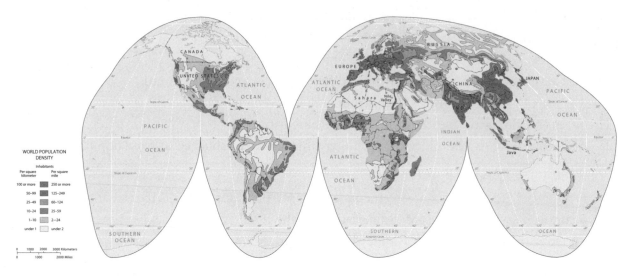

© H. J. de Blij, P. O. Muller, and John Wiley & Sons, Inc.

According to the map on pages 44–45, World Population Density, which of the following statements is accurate?

A. the Western Hemisphere has a majority of the densest locations in the world

B. the further away you go from the equator, the more dense the population becomes

C. East Asia's density issue is due to lack of family planning options

D. coastal areas and those along rivers tend to contain larger population densities than the interior

E. Canada's population density is oriented to markets in China

KEY FOR QUESTIONS:

1) A
2) B
3) E
4) E
5) A
6) C
7) D

SECTION 2
REVIEWING FREE RESPONSE QUESTIONS

Quick Review: There are three Free Response Questions (FRQs) on the AP Human Geography exam. We imagine that your teachers will work with you throughout the year with FRQs as assessments. Whether you read this at the beginning of the year or at the end of the year, it matters not. If you read this at the end of the year, consider this a review of the key elements of writing an effective FRQ. If you read this at the beginning of the year, consider this a preview on how to succeed during the year. (And if you read this in the beginning and the end of the year, you really need to get outside more.)

OBEY THE SPEED LIMIT

Before we give you an example of a FRQ, you need to learn (or review) how to actively read an FRQ. Knowing how to actively read an FRQ will help you perform better on the APHG exam. Too many students speed-read through the question only to get it wrong because they didn't read it correctly. In our minds, the worst thing that could happen is giving a great answer to the wrong question because you didn't read it correctly. So, slow down………

FRQ RULES!!

Remember that these are FRQs. That stands for FREE RESPONSE QUESTION. So, it is a QUESTION to which you will RESPOND in a FREE manner. That is, you have a lot of flexibility in the way you write your responses. A well-written APHG FRQ contains solid geographic information. There are no style rules as some other AP courses have. So, RESPOND FREELY to the QUESTION, making sure you provide what the question is asking.

Here are the first things you need to understand about FRQs:

#1 The questions usually begin with an opening statement:

This basically gives you a background for the question—it creates a framework.

#2 FRQs are multipart questions:

There is always at least an "A" and a "B" to an FRQ Question.

#3 Look for the key verbs:

THIS IS THE MOST IMPORTANT THING YOU WILL DO!!! If you look for the key verbs in the question, you'll know what you specifically need to do in the question. This is so IMPORTANT, we will dedicate more writing to it below.

#4 Underline and highlight other key words:

Once you find the key verbs, then you want to underline the other key terms in the question. Terms are going to be very important, but other words that help indicate what you need to do are also important. Conjunctions like "and" or "or" are extremely important. Also, numbers play a major role in what you need to do. So, if it states "define TWO terms," make sure you write about two and not just one. In fact, it is important for you to know that only the number of examples requested in the question are scored on the exam. For example, if the question asks for two examples, only the first two examples you provide will be scored. Any subsequent examples will NOT be scored. The bottom line is, just read and follow the exam instructions.

#5 Responses to FRQs are not five paragraph themes:

You DO NOT need to write an introduction, body, and conclusion to a question as a response. Writing in complete sentences is essential. However, an FRQ is not an English essay. We want you to just answer the question.

LAW and ORDER: KVU (Key Verbs Unit)

Have you ever watched any of the versions of the television show *Law and Order*? Each show always starts with a crime scene. The detectives look over the crime scene to see what they can learn about what happened and formulate hypotheses. Well, we will do that in our next section titled ***"So What Does an APHG Free Response Question (FRQ) Look Like"?*** But for now let's send the questions (or staying with our *Law and Order* theme—the body) over to the coroner for an autopsy.

Okay, not to sound morbid, but the cause of "death" on many student FRQ answers is not being able to find the key verbs. We really do want you to learn how to watch for key words–especially certain verbs—what we like to call the "operative action verbs." Wow! They sound important and they are. So here goes the autopsy of APHG FRQs.

Between 2001 and 2012, the APHG exam used the following verbs this many times:

Verb Used	Number of Uses, 2001–2012
Define	8
Identify	21
Describe	6
Analyze	1
Discuss	19
Explain	36
Name/Give/Support/List	8
Give a Detailed Account	1
Apply	2
Predict	1

Data collated from: http://apcentral.collegeboard.com/apc/members/exam/exam_information/2004.html

What we need to do is look at the verbs used and the relative complexity or length needed for each response based on the verb used—if only there was a chart that could indicate the response complexity and length. Well, here is such a chart! Study each verb and the number of times it has been used. Also study what that verb means and look to see how you can use that verb when answering a FRQ.

KEY VERBS TO UNLOCK THE APHG FREE RESPONSE QUESTIONS*

Response Complexity & Length	Verb/Action/What to Do	How Much to Write?
	IDENTIFY – NAME – DEFINE – LIST – SUPPORT WITH	**A sentence, two, or three**
	DESCRIBE – APPLY – GIVE A DETAILED ACCOUNT	**String some sentences together**
	EXPLAIN – APPLY	**Write a paragraph**
	ANALYZE	**String paragraphs together**
	DISCUSS – PREDICT	**Write a page or two**

NEVER, EVER, EVER WRITE YOUR ANSWERS IN BULLET FORM
* Verbs used on APHG Exam FRQs 2001-2011
Data collated from: http://apcentral.collegeboard.com/apc/members/exam/exam_information/2004.html

And as the font size and arrow indicate, the further down or larger, you need to go more in depth at the bottom than at the top.

We're almost ready to show you a sample FRQ. But we really want you to understand the above chart. So, let's divide the chart up into two groups: **laid-back action verbs** and **high-maintenance action verbs**.

The Laid-Back Action Verbs

1. Define: Give the meaning of (a word or phrase)
2. Identify/Name: Establish or indicate what something is
3. List: Give a series of names, words, or other items
4. Describe: Give an account in words of (someone or something), including all the relevant characteristics, qualities, or events

TRANSLATION: Write a definition, give examples, list characteristics, and so on. These verbs mean you should write a sentence or two sentences or three sentences.

The second series of verbs is more complex and is asking for a much deeper understanding of concepts. Yes, these are our high-maintenance action verbs. Typically, responses to questions with these verbs will be longer and more complex. These terms are as follows:

The High-Maintenance Action Verbs

1. Analyze: to examine in detail the structure of something, especially for purposes of explanation and interpretation
2. Discuss: to write about a topic in detail, taking into account different ideas and opinions
3. Explain: to make an idea, situation, or problem clear by describing it in more detail or revealing relevant facts or ideas

TRANSLATION: Tear things down into pieces, make judgments about what works and what does not (yes, criticize a model as one example), tell how things are the same and different.
   You are writing at least a paragraph and possibly more.
   Discuss—this means write a paragraph or two.
   Explain—this means write some paragraphs and string them together.

Probably the best thing we can do for you right now is give you an example of a Free Response Question. Now, as you read the question, the first thing you should do is find the VERBS—THESE ARE THE KEY WORDS TO SUCCESS ON THE FRQ.

Sample FRQ:

Immigration has been a part of the history of the United States from its earliest roots. The chart on page 109 of the text lists a general pattern of immigration from 1821 to 2000.

A. Define the following terms:
   1. Migration
   2. Forced Migration
   3. Selective Migration

> B. Describe the difference between a "push" factor and a "pull" factor and explain how each has
>   occurred using one specific example of each with reference to the chart above.
> C. With reference to the map, explain in detail two reasons associated with declines in
>   immigration during a specific time period.

Dissecting the Sample Free Response Question (FRQ)

As we stated on page 181–182, there are five things you need to learn about an FRQ. Let's dissect the question by looking at all five of those components.

#1 The questions usually start with an opening statement:

We have an opening statement, but is it really telling you anything you couldn't figure out on your own? Nope. Again, the purpose of the opening statement is to frame the question and help you "get in the zone." Cover up the opening statement. Could you still answer the question? You betcha! Well, as long as you studied the material.

#2 FRQs are multipart questions:

There is always an "A," "B," and "C" section to this question. Typically you'll see questions with two or three parts, occasionally there are four-part questions. In order to receive full credit, you must answer all three parts.

PLEASE NOTE: On AP exams, you don't know how much each section is weighted and they may or may not be equal. Therefore, answer each part of the exam as though it were weighted equally. That way, you will be striving for maximum credit regardless of how many points each section is worth.

#3 Look for the key verbs:

It's pretty simple to find the word "define" in part A. And "describe" in part B is just as easy. "Explain" in part C is a little harder, but it can be done. These words truly tell you what you need to do. But, wait. Did you see that there is one more OPERATIVE ACTION VERB in part B? How can it be? Let's go to the next section and explain.

#4 Underline and highlight other key words:

Look at part B of the question. There is one other word that is essentially the next important word after the OPERATIVE ACTION VERBS.

Hopefully, you see that the word is "and" AND it is used twice. Both times the use of the term is extremely important. The second "and" links a second operative action verb into the fold: explain. So, in essence, you have two actions in Part B. But, wait, there's more. The first "and" effectively splits the first action into two parts. And, simple math (2 x 2 = 4) will show you that you have 4 steps in part B.

Now look at Part C. After the OPERATIVE ACTION VERB, can you find the next important word? The word is "two."

We think there are other words that are important, such as terms.

In fact, on the next page we have restated the question with key terms highlighted. We have boxed the operative action verbs, circled conjunctions and numbers, and finally, underlined the other key terms.

#5 Responses to FRQs are not five paragraph themes:

Let's look at Part A. There is no need for an introduction or conclusion. Just give the definitions and give them in complete sentences. Really, could you imagine writing an introduction:

"There are many terms used to describe immigration and migration. I will successfully define three specific terms detailing with immigration: migration, forced migration, and selective migration."

Boring—and a time waster. Just write in complete sentences, as the exam instructions dictate. A very acceptable practice (and a good idea) would be to actually underline the term you were defining.

Look at Part C again. An acceptable practice (and another good idea) would be to list your two points by starting with "1" and "2."

Example:

C. (1) One reason immigration declined in the 1930s was the Great Depression.
   With unemployment soaring, America was no longer a source for jobs.

   (2) Immigration also declined in the 1930s because of quotas imposed by such legislative acts as the National Origins Law. These quotas limited the number of immigrants allowed into the United States. Many of these laws were motivated by politicians who blamed immigration for high unemployment in the United States.

Sample FRQ with key words indicated:

1) Immigration has been a part of the history of the United States from its earliest roots. The chart above (p. 104) lists a general pattern of immigration from 1821 to 2000.

   A)   Define the following terms:

   1.   Migration
   2.   Forced Migration
   3.   Selective Migration

   B. Describe the difference between a "push" factor and a "pull" factor and explain how each has occurred using one specific example of each with reference to the chart above.

   C. With reference to the map, explain in detail two reasons associated with declines in immigration during a specific time period.

KEY:

• Verbs: ▭

• Conjunctions and Numbers: ◯

• Other Key Words: ___

Source: Gregory Sherwin.

Here is the sample FRQ with the key words highlighted:

Read the question with just the highlighted words. A bit confusing? Perhaps, but we think you could answer the question effectively if you knew just those words. Notice we didn't highlight any of the words in the opening statement. We suppose you could and the opening statement is helpful, but we feel it isn't essential to answering the question.

THE NITTY GRITTY

Now that we have looked at key verbs and a sample question, let's combine those ideas into the different types of questions that are asked as a whole—with real AP examples for each.

We've come up with clever titles for all these different types of questions (based on pop culture) as a way to help you organize your ideas. Enjoy them if you like; create your own new titles if you prefer. Just learn them!!! Here we go.

THE TRANSFORMER QUESTION

APHG FRQs aren't exactly like the Transformers you might have played with as a child—but you do remember how those robots that transformed into cars or morphed into something really cool?

However, just like those toy Transformers, this type of question morphs as you go along.

A Transformer question is basically a definition question. This type of question asks you to **define a term or concept** and **give *specific* examples and explanations.**

In this type of question, you might be asked to do the following:

Part A—Define geographic vocabulary, concepts, theories, or models.

Part B—A definition alone will not allow you to score well. You may be asked to give one, two, or more real-world examples of the definition(s) in Part A.

Part C—You might be asked to USE or APPLY the definitions and examples geographically from Parts A and B.

A Transformer-type question is designed to get more difficult as you go from Part A to Part B to Part C and so on. In other words, you should clearly define whatever is asked in Part A and then supply more details in Part C than you did in Part B.

So, the idea or hope is that everyone should get some points by defining the term. But the rubber hits the road as the question moves forward.

What we are saying is that Part A is designed so that most students can answer it. Part B is designed to see who can relate the geographic term, theory, or concept to the real world. Part C allows the student to demonstrate proficiency in analyzing and applying the geographic concept spatially.

Examples of Transformer Questions
2002 Exam – Question 1
2011 Exam – Question 1

Please go to: http://apcentral.collegeboard.com/apc/members/exam/exam_information/2004.html to find these questions.

THE GROUNDHOG DAY QUESTION

Do you remember this classic movie? Phil Connors (played by Bill Murray) kept waking up to the same day in the movie *Groundhog Day* over and over and over.

This next type of question is a little bit like that.

A Groundhog Day question asks you to make **connections** between and among different spatial concepts. In these questions, you are being asked to analyze a prompt and to apply geographic/spatial knowledge and concepts. The *Groundhog Day* part is that you will have A, B, C, and D items* that you will answer back multiple times through the original prompt.

This type of question asks you to **connect** your geographic knowledge (connections to a **scenario, case studies, real-world situations, etc.**) to the question prompt. In other words, you will answer Part A using the prompt. Then, you will go back to the prompt and answer Part B, C, and so on. Now do you see the *Groundhog Day* connection?

A connection-type question is a bit more difficult for most students. You should fully explain every part of an answer in a connection question. Poor answers on this question tend to come from those who give only rudimentary information. Students who score well on this type of question can tie *seemingly* nongeographic information to the prompt. In other words, good students make geographic connections between things that, on the surface, appear unrelated.

Examples
2001 Exam – Question 2
2005 Exam – Question 3

---

*The number of actual letters in the question will vary. It could be A, B; or A, B, C; or A, B, C, D.

Please go to: http://apcentral.collegeboard.com/apc/members/exam/exam_information/2004.html to find these questions.

THE "MOTHER OF ALL QUESTIONS" QUESTION

In 1991, Saddam Hussein declared that Iraq was engaged in the "Mother of All Battles" against United States-led coalition forces in the Persian Gulf War. His declaration, though obviously overstated (and, it didn't work out so well for Saddam), is used here to make a point and gets at the next type of question.

When you deal with "the mother of all questions," you're going to get hit with a lot of fire power. Here comes a **synthetic, process-oriented, critical thinking question** all at once. You wanna duck, but you can't. Now, it is true that all APHG questions have some process and critical thinking components in them. But, this type of question is designed to get you thinking, analyzing and putting things together in spatial ways.

A "Mother of All Questions" question requires you to analyze the question and write a synthetic answer using geographic/spatial knowledge and skills. The synthetic question involves taking complex concepts, explaining these concepts, pulling in diverse pieces of information, and developing a process-oriented answer. To be successful on this question, you must remain highly focused on the prompts. That is, you must keep weaving a discussion, which continues to build on the previous points. Good answers on a synthetic question are those where you string together information you have learned from three, four, five, or even more chapters/units from the course.

Examples
2002 Exam – Question 3
2006 Exam – Question 2

Please go to: http://apcentral.collegeboard.com/apc/members/exam/exam_information/2004.html to find these questions.

FINAL ADVICE

1. FEAR NOT (our apologies to the prophet Isaiah)!!

Also, don't be afraid to call things into question when answering APHG questions. For example, on the first APHG exam in 2001 students were asked to write (in part) about the "usefulness" of a particular geographic model. The word *usefulness* implies that the student could (and should) evaluate that model using real-world examples. Using acceptable arguments, you could validate the model, call the model's assumptions into question, or refute the model as outdated, impractical, or wrong. The synthetic question really gives you a chance to shine, be creative, and draw from the multiple experiences of an APHG class. Knowledge from the text, field trips, web exercises, supplemental readings, research projects, applied current events, and personal experiences could be used to answer a synthetic question.

2. STAR TREK

Remember, this is your chance to use every part of the course to construct a good answer. Now, go boldly where no man has gone before (you do realize this *Star Trek* quote is the world's most famous split infinitive—but that's for your AP Language class) and write synthetically!

FINAL REMINDERS FOR SUCCESS ON THE APHG EXAM

The following is a list of best practices for the day before and day of the APHG exam. Rules, conditions, and situations in your particular school or testing center may vary. But, we believe if you follow these suggestions, you will create opportunities to do well on the APHG exam.

Ø   NO CELL PHONES IN THE TESTING ROOM—Leave them in your car or locker. Some schools and testing centers will take them up for you at the door. Just do not have them with you when taking the exam. Having a phone in the exam room/center can result in you having your test scores cancelled.

Ø   Get plenty of sleep the night before the exam.

Ø   Eat a protein-rich breakfast. Protein fires up your brain and can help you get ready to think.

Ø   Be on time for the exam—be 10 minutes early. Some testing centers will lock the doors and not allow you to enter if you are late.

Ø   Bring #2 pencils and black or dark blue pens—erasable if desired. Pencils are used on the MCQs and pens are used on the FRQs.

Ø   The MCQ section is first, has 75 questions, and is 60 minutes in length.

Ø   Do not linger over an MCQ item—if you read it a few times and have not answered it, go on to the next item. Remember to circle items that cause difficulty or that you leave blank so you can come back to them later.

Ø   Be careful with NOT and EXCEPT items. In other words, read carefully as all the answers on these items are correct except for one.

Ø   If you have any time remaining and you have finished the MCQs, go back and check your answers for accuracy.

Ø   ALWAYS go back and check MCQs with stimulus material. This gives you a chance to check your answer on the questions with maps, photos, diagrams, and so on.

Ø   Remember, when the APHG exam is over, you may NEVER discuss the MCQs! You signed an agreement to this extent when the APHG exam began.

Ø   THERE WILL BE A 15-minute BREAK AFTER THE MCQs.

Ø   At the break get up, walk around, go outside. Get your blood flowing and clear your head. You still have the other half of the exam to take.

Ø   Be on time coming back after the break.

Ø   On FRQs, apply the techniques taught to you.

Ø   The FRQ section is three questions with 75 minutes to answer.

Ø   For up to 5 minutes, read all three FRQs and make a short outline or write down key words to help with possible answers.

Ø   Determine which questions you consider the easiest to most difficult to answer.

Ø   Do not go over this 1- minute time frame.

Ø   When finished answering your easy question, attack the next easiest question and allow 15-20 minutes to answer it.

Ø   Do not go over this 20-minute time frame.

Ø   Finally, attack the last question, allowing 25-30 minutes to answer it.

Ø   Do not go over this 30-minute time frame.

Ø   If you use all of the maximum time here, you will still have 5 minutes left over. It is likely you will have a lot more time left.

Ø   Use any remaining time to review answers and/or add items to your answers.

Additional Tips

Ø   Always skip space between FRQs.

Ø   Be sure not to write your answers on the exam questions. Always write your answers in the blank pages provided.

AP HUMAN GEOGRAPHY
EXAM ONE

You should allow 60 minutes to choose the BEST answer for each of the following items.

1. Which branch of geography focuses upon natural landforms, climate, soils, and vegetation of the Earth?
   a. cultural geography
   b. human geography
   c. locational geography
   d. physical geography
   e. political geography

Use the quote from a National Council for Geographic Education newsletter, *Perspective*, to answer the following question.

> The following is a quote from *Geography in the News* reported in September 2003: "The SARS (Severe Acute Respiratory Syndrome) virus is a highly contagious disease. New infections seem to radiate out from the epicenter. However, the virus may leapfrog to new centers, as infected individuals travel along transportation routes to other cities and towns. Rural residents with few contacts with major cities tend to avoid the virus until nearly the end of its diffusion cycle."

2. According to the reading, SARS affects rural residents in what appears to be BEST described as a form of _____ diffusion.
   a. stimulus
   b. hierarchical
   c. reverse hierarchical
   d. voluntary
   e. contagious

3.   The map below, known for its distortion of the high latitudes, is a(n):

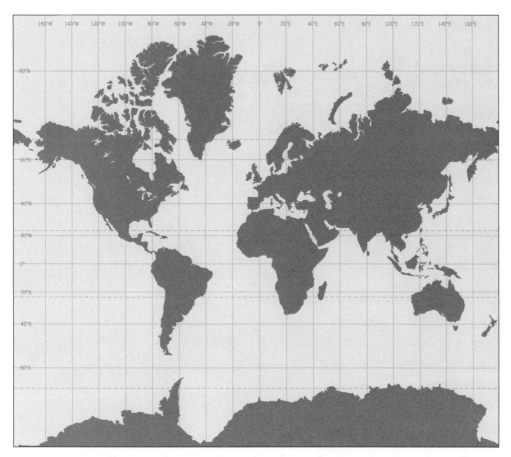

From Fouberg, Murphy, and de Blij, *Human Geography, Tenth Edition*, John Wiley & Sons, Inc.

    a.   Robinson projection
    b.   Mercator projection
    c.   Isopleth
    d.   Equal Area projection
    e.   Cartogram

4.   The location of a place in relationship to other places or features around it is called:
    a.   absolute location
    b.   site location
    c.   relative location
    d.   actual location
    e.   perceived location

5.   The diagram below best indicates the concept of:

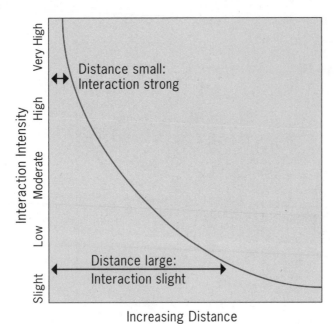

© E. H. Fouberg, A. B. Murphy, H. J. de Blij, and John Wiley & Sons, Inc.

    a.   hierarchical diffusion

    b.   assimilation

    c.   barriers to diffusion

    d.   distance decay

    e.   acculturation

6.   Mental (or cognitive) maps are largely:

    a.   accurate and reflect actual information on printed maps

    b.   made up of cartographic and physiologic information

    c.   an accurate analysis of accessible data

    d.   based on imagined experiences of an individual

    e.   largely developed from first-hand experiences in a place

7.   The layering of geographic data by computers into data sets is known as:

    a.   GPS

    b.   ENSO

    c.   RSS

    d.   GIS

    e.   GNI

8.   Which map projection is exhibited below?

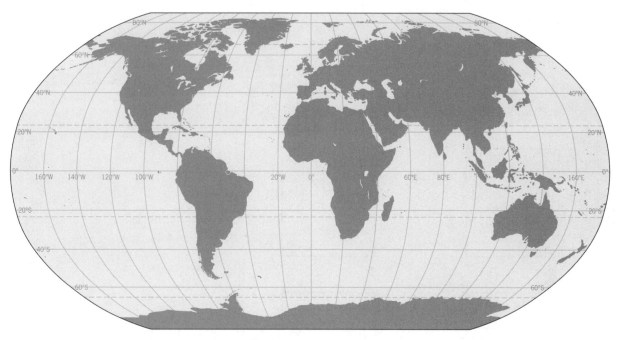

From Fouberg, Murphy, and de Blij, *Human Geography, Tenth Edition*, John Wiley & Sons, Inc.

a.   Mercator
b.   Goode's Interrupted
c.   Robinson
d.   Cartogram
e.   Choropleth

9.   Which of the following statements about migration is INCORRECT?
a.   Many migrants leave their homes because of war.
b.   Environmental problems cause many people to migrate.
c.   Most migrants leave their homes because of high taxes.
d.   Many migrants go to poor countries that cannot accommodate more people.
e.   Most migrants in the world leave to pursue a "better life."

10.   The approximate growth rate needed to sustain replacement of a population is:
a.   5.8%
b.   7.1%
c.   10.5%
d.   4.6%
e.   2.1%

11. Using your knowledge of population density and distribution, which two of the four boxes have the highest *density* of triangles?
    a. 1, 3
    b. 3, 4
    c. 1, 2
    d. 4, 1
    e. 2, 3

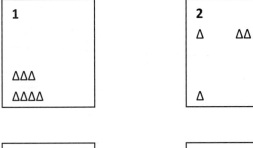

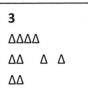
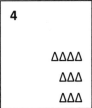

12. The world's population can best be described as generally concentrated in:
    a. East Asia and Southern Europe
    b. Northwestern North America and South Asia
    c. South Asia and East Asia
    d. Europe and Eastern South America
    e. Western Africa and Southeast Asia

13. Contrary to the predictions of Malthus in 1798, food production has since grown exponentially because of all of the following EXCEPT:
    a. Green Revolution
    b. mechanization
    c. technology
    d. genetic engineering
    e. increased farm land

14. The statistic that reports the number of deaths per thousand people in a given year in a population is called:
    a. total fecundity or fertility rate
    b. crude death or mortality rate
    c. adjusted population level
    d. actual growth rate
    e. age-sex mortality rate

15. Assuming the Demographic Transition Model has five stages, the actual *transition* is represented by:
    a. stages three and four
    b. stages one and two
    c. stages two and three
    d. stages one and three
    e. stages one and five

16. Population growth is exceptionally fast from both migration and total fertility in which of the following cities?
    a. Lagos
    b. London
    c. New York City
    d. Tokyo
    e. Paris

17. One of historical geography's major examples of agriculturally induced migration involved the movement of hundreds of thousands of citizens to the U.S. from which European country in the 1830s & 1840s?
    a. Ireland
    b. England
    c. Belgium
    d. Spain
    e. Greece

18. One of the "laws" of migration as derived by Ravenstein states that:
    a. urban residents are more migratory than inhabitants of rural areas
    b. urban residents tend to be less religious than rural residents
    c. rural inhabitants hardly ever migrate
    d. urban residents are less migratory than inhabitants of rural areas
    e. rural people tend to farm more than urban people

19. A family decided to move to another region or place a long distance away, but finds a suitable place to settle before reaching their original intended destination. This is called:
    a. temporary settlement
    b. luck option
    c. intervening opportunity
    d. reverse distance decay
    e. sequent occupance

20. The number of deaths per 1000 population between the first and fifth birthdays is known as:
    a. natural increase rate
    b. infant mortality rate
    c. crude death rate
    d. total death rate
    e. child mortality rate

21. A country that has reached a stage where the population has very low growth, such as Germany or Japan, should have a population pyramid that is _____ -shaped.
    a. bell
    b. apple
    c. rectangular
    d. pyramid
    e. circular

22. From the list below, choose the country with the most languages spoken.
    a. China
    b. Brazil
    c. India
    d. Pakistan
    e. Canada

23. The two theories of the Proto-Indo European language dispersal through Europe are the conquest theory and the _____ theory.
    a. agriculture
    b. migration
    c. trade routes
    d. missionary
    e. technology

24. As of 2003, the largest ethnic minority group in the United States is now:
    a. Asians
    b. Hispanics
    c. Turks
    d. Native Americans
    e. Americans of African ancestry

25. Any common language spoken by peoples of diverse speech is today called a/an:
    a. official language
    b. monolingual language
    c. pidgin language
    d. lingua franca
    e. idiomatic tongue

26. The island in the Mediterranean Sea that had to be partitioned because two cultures, the Greeks and Turks, could not get along is:
    a. Malta
    b. Sicily
    c. Corsica
    d. Sardinia
    e. Cyprus

27. The branch of Christianity that has been resurrected in Russia, Eastern Europe and many Slavic countries and is growing rapidly is:
    a. Catholicism
    b. Protestantism
    c. Eastern Orthodox
    d. Shaker
    e. Unitarianism

28. Islam dominates in:
    a. Southeast and East Asia
    b. South Asia and South Africa
    c. West and Central Africa
    d. Northern Africa and Southwest Asia
    e. Sub-Saharan Africa and South America

29. By the late 1990s, the fastest growing of the world religions had become:
    a.   Christianity
    b.   Islam
    c.   Buddhism
    d.   Hinduism
    e.   Judaism

30. A simplified form of a lingua franca is known as a(n):
    a.   pidgin
    b.   euphemism
    c.   Creole
    d.   dialect
    e.   idiom

31. Which of the following supports the following position statement: *English will continue to be the global lingua franca in the year 2100.*
    a.   Total Fertility Rates among English-speaking peoples are generally low.
    b.   There are many linguistic revival movements going on around the world today.
    c.   The computer/internet allows non-English languages more opportunity for diffusion.
    d.   English is the international language of business, travel and air traffic control.
    e.   Many countries have enacted laws to limit the use of English in their country.

32. Sikhism is a religion that arose from the confrontation between:
    a.   Buddhism and Islam
    b.   Islam and Hinduism
    c.   Christianity and Islam
    d.   Judaism and Hinduism
    e.   Hinduism and Buddhism

33. Hinduism has not spread by expansion diffusion in modern times, but at one time it did spread by relocation diffusion as a result of:
    a.   the transportation of Indian workers abroad during the colonial period
    b.   conquest by militant groups from Sri Lanka
    c.   forced relocation by due invaders from the North
    d.   massive voluntary emigrations due to pull factors of Hinduism
    e.   India's colonies in the East Africa realms

34. Nigeria is a multilingual country with many tribal boundaries where Christianity prevails in the south and _____ in the north.
    a. Judaism
    b. Buddhism
    c. Sikhism
    d. Hinduism
    e. Islam

35. Using your mental maps and not thinking in terms of numbers of adherents of each religion, which of the following world religions is the LEAST widely diffused?
    a. Buddhism
    b. Christianity
    c. Islam
    d. Judaism
    e. Hinduism

36. Which of the following countries has not passed a national law based on protecting a language?
    a. Canada
    b. United States
    c. Belgium
    d. France
    e. Romania

37. Which of the following is a reason for different countries in the same region having similar words for the word milk?
    a. language divergence
    b. language convergence
    c. language extinction
    d. language obstruction
    e. language commodification

Photo by Paul Gray

38. The sign above shows which geographic concept?
    a. linguistic revitalization
    b. religious syncretism
    c. language convergence
    d. universal religion
    e. lingua franca

39. A federal state:
    a. has an unusually strong central government which controls the whole state equally
    b. is usually very large geographically and therefore may have very diverse peoples
    c. does not allow for the regional and cultural interests of minority groups
    d. is most likely to have very few, if any, sub-state units
    e. always has a capital city that is located in the middle of the country

40. Political states that have a religious government are known as:
    a. atheistic
    b. theocratic
    c. mercantile
    d. egalitarian
    e. nucleated

41. Which of the following is in the correct order regarding the establishment of boundaries?
    a.   define – delimit – demarcate
    b.   delimit – define – demarcate
    c.   demarcate – delimit – define
    d.   delimit – demarcate – define
    e.   define – demarcate - delimit

42. In which of the following state morphologies is internal circulation/transportation/contact or other friction of distance issue *most* likely to be a major problem?
    a.   fragmented
    b.   compact
    c.   perforated
    d.   enclave
    e.   prorupted

43. Which of the following phrases BEST defines "stateless nation"?
    a.   many ethnic groups within several contiguous states with no one group dominating
    b.   a group of people with a common culture and sense of unity but with no territory
    c.   a single nation dispersed across and predominant in two or more states
    d.   distinct group of people occupying their own territory & sharing a common set of values
    e.   an independent political entity that is not subdivided into regional or local units.

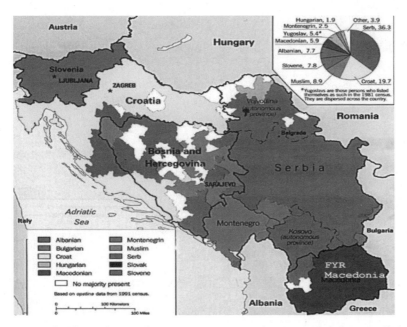

From de Blij and Murphy, *Human Geography, Seventh Edition*, John Wiley & Sons, Inc.

44. Which of the following concepts does the map on page 205 best highlight?
    a. gerrymandering
    b. reapportionment
    c. shatterbelt
    d. neocolonialism
    e. annexation

45. _____ is the redistricting of Congressional seats according to population after
    each census.
    a. Supranationalism
    b. Gerrymandering
    c. Majority-minority
    d. Reapportionment
    e. Federal

46. Which of the following is the BEST example of a set of stateless nations on the international
    stage?
    a. Basques – Palestinians – Kurds
    b. Cherokee – Sioux – Choctaw
    c. Lithuanians – Latvians – Estonians
    d. Thais – Vietnamese – Cambodians
    e. Bengalis – Burmese – Bhutanese

47. Organic theory postulates that the state's essential, life-giving force is:
    a. population
    b. a strong military
    c. mobility
    d. territory
    e. power

48. Which of the following devolution groups/movements does not match with
    country/countries?
    a. Catalonians – Spain
    b. Slovenians, Croatians, Bosnians – Yugoslavia
    c. Walloons/Flemish – Belgium
    d. Basques – Spain/France
    e. Sicilians –Greece

49. Efforts by three or more countries who give up some measure of sovereignty to forge associations for common advantage and goals is known as:
    a.   superinternationalism
    b.   internationalism
    c.   supranationalism
    d.   intranationalism
    e.   neocolonialism

50. The Peace of Westphalia is MOST important to the study of political geography because it:
    a.   was the treaty that ended the Thirty Years War
    b.   finally helped the French make peace with Germany
    c.   contained language that recognized the formation of states
    d.   organized the first example of supranationalism
    e.   opened talks between the Ottoman Turks and Portugal

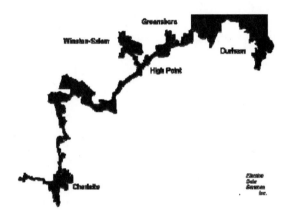

Reproduced with permission from Election Data Services, Inc.

51. The map of a North Carolina Congressional District above is indicative of:
    a.   geometric boundaries
    b.   supranationalism
    c.   gerrymandering
    d.   devolution
    e.   core-peripheries

52. The motives for most examples of supranational cooperation, such as NAFTA and MERCOSUR by the late 1990s were:
    a.   mutual defense
    b.   ethnic identification
    c.   economic
    d.   religious
    e.   linguistic

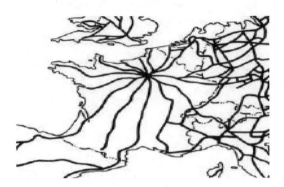

Murphy, A. B.; Jordan-Bychkov, Terry G.; and Jordan, Bella Bychdova. *The European Culture Area: A Systematic Geography*, 5th ed. (Lanham, MD and Boulder, CO: Rowman & Littlefield, 2009), p. 168.

53. The map of major roads above most likely shows a _____.
    a. microstate
    b. fragmented state
    c. federal state
    d. perforated state
    e. unitary state

54. The extractive sector is also known as the _____ sector, while the service sector is also known as the _____ sector.
    a. secondary; quinary
    b. tertiary; secondary
    c. primary; tertiary
    d. quaternary; primary
    e. quinary; quaternary

55. Which of the following is CORRECT with regard to plant origins?
    a. Southeast Asia – watermelon, bamboo, beans
    b. Mesoamerica – maize (corn), squash, beans
    c. Southwest Asia – millets, water chestnuts, peanuts
    d. Eastern India – tomatoes, potatoes, okra
    e. Ethiopian and East African Highlands – rice, bananas, bamboo

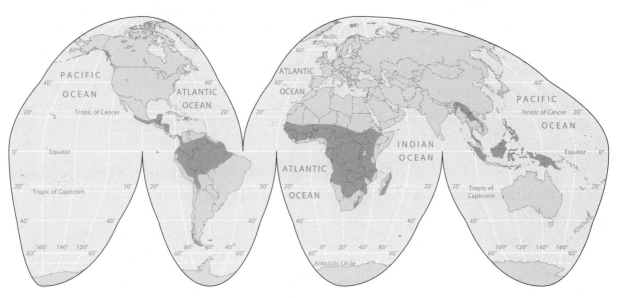

© E. H. Fouberg, A. B. Murphy, H. J. de Blij, and John Wiley & Sons, Inc.

56. The shaded areas on the map above most likely depict which of the following types of agricultural practice?
    a. livestocking
    b. commercial
    c. hydroponics
    d. subsistence
    e. dairying

Use the following excerpt from the *New York Times* World section – January 25, 2008 issue to answer the question below.

   Instead of counting on free markets to generate opportunities spontaneously, the nonprofit groups managing some of the grants will intervene to help farmers form groups to sell goods in bulk and provide them with access to the agronomic advice, processing facilities and transportation they need to take advantage of growing markets for products like milk and coffee. In Kenya, Rwanda and Uganda, for example, Heifer International—working with other groups and institutions—will help women who tend cows gain access to refrigeration plants, enabling them to sell milk for distribution to stores distant from their farms."

57. Which of following best exemplifies the agricultural issues in the quote above?
    a. von Thünen's model has been made partially obsolete
    b. Kenyan farmers are vertically integrating agribusiness
    c. extensive commercial agriculture in the developing world
    d. shift from traditional agriculture to agribusiness
    e. women in Kenya are becoming plantation farmers

58. The integration of the Roman Empire was greatly facilitated by a:
    a.   road system
    b.   lack of different languages
    c.   conurbation effort
    d.   lack of foreign enemies
    e.   good postal system

59. _____ describes a city's position relative to much-traveled transport routes, production of farmland, and manufacturing and other towns/cities.
    a.   Site
    b.   Nucleation
    c.   Exurbanization
    d.   Situation
    e.   Rank-size

60. Urban Hierarchy from the bottom up is best described by which of the following?
    a.   Village – Hamlet – City – Town – Metropolis
    b.   Hamlet – Town – City – Metropolis – Megalopolis
    c.   Town – Village – Hamlet – City – Metropolis
    d.   Hamlet – City – Town – Village – Megalopolis
    e.   Megalopolis – Metropolis – City – Town – Hamlet

61. Which of the following is LEAST correct regarding professional sports and urban geography?
    a.   Higher order functions such as professional sports teams are usually located at the top of the rank-size hierarchy.
    b.   Smaller cities usually have professional sports teams because they have the most loyal and rabid fans.
    c.   Professional sports teams have both multiplied since 1950 and diffused to the South and the West in the US.
    d.   The NHL has diffused to the Southern and Western states following the general shift in US population.
    e.   Having professional sports teams is seen as part of what being an important city.

62. Which of the following is a CORRECT statement concerning the *spacing* of human settlements?
    a.   Villages are separated by great distances.
    b.   Large cities tend to be closer together than smaller ones.
    c.   Towns are farther apart than cities.
    d.   Large cities tend to be farther apart than smaller cities.
    e.   A megalopolis tends to be geographically small.

63. The greatest number of workers in a city or town's economic base is in the:
   a.   agricultural sector
   b.   basic sector
   c.   quasi-basic sector
   d.   manufacturing sector
   e.   nonbasic sector

64. _____ is the rehabilitation of deteriorated inner city areas.
   a.   Commercialization
   b.   Suburbanization
   c.   Gesellschaft
   d.   Nucleation
   e.   Gentrification

© Rob Crandall/The Image Works.

65. This photo most likely shows a(n) _____ of a large metropolitan CBD.
   a.   megalopolis
   b.   edge city
   c.   village
   d.   ethnic neighborhood
   e.   tenement

66. Core countries are characterized by all of the following EXCEPT:
    a. high metals consumption
    b. low employment in agriculture
    c. high caloric diet
    d. low protein intake
    e. high literacy rates

67. Which of the following is an example of a business/industry in the primary sector?
    a. a chewing gum factory
    b. an iron ore mine
    c. an insurance company
    d. a private university
    e. a call center

68. Theory declares that prosperity is sustained in the core, while poverty is sustained in the periphery:
    a. Organic
    b. Modernization
    c. Dependency
    d. Secondary
    e. Time-Space Convergence

69. Which of the factors of industrial location below is inaccurate?
    a. The periphery must sell raw materials to the core to procure foreign capital and currency.
    b. The core keeps prices of desired goods low by switching from supplier to supplier in the periphery.
    c. Low wages mean lower-priced goods and lead to flooded markets of cheaply priced goods.
    d. Highly developed industrial centers have highly developed transport systems.
    e. Transport costs tend to be a minimally important factor that a firm considers in location.

70. Which of the following transportation distance/cost to transportation mode associations is CORRECT?
    a. Short – Water
    b. Intermediate – Railroad
    c. Long – Truck
    d. Intermediate – Water
    e. Short – Air

71. According to Rostow's Model, highly developed countries are in stages:
    a.   3 and 4
    b.   1 and 2
    c.   2, 3 and 4
    d.   5 and 1
    e.   4 and 5

72. Proximity to the market is more significant in industrial location when the commodity/finished product is:
    a.   small and/or fragile
    b.   high in value
    c.   bulky and/or heavy
    d.   low in value
    e.   small and/or expensive

73. Among the significant recent innovations in bulk transport is the development of:
    a.   container systems
    b.   pipeline systems
    c.   better railroad lines
    d.   more efficient trucks
    e.   air freight

74. Weber did for industry as von Thünen did for agriculture by predicting ways to minimize costs. What were the three basic costs Weber focused on minimizing?
    a.   labor – deglomeration – other factors
    b.   transportation – labor – excise taxes
    c.   agglomeration – transportation – labor
    d.   labor – food costs – transportation
    e.   raw materials – agglomeration – owner preference

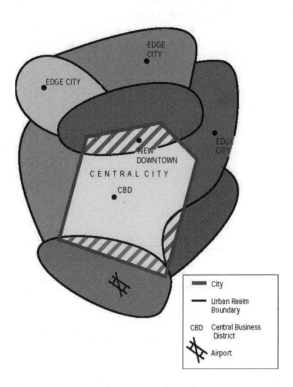

From Murphy, de Blij, and Fouberg, *Human Geography, Eighth Edition*, John Wiley and Sons, Inc. Adapted with permission from: T. Hartshorn and P. O. Muller, "Suburban Downtowns and the Transformation of Metropolitan Atlanta's Business Landscape," *Urban Geography* 10 (1989), p. 375.

75. Which of the urban models is shown above?
    a.   Central Place Theory
    b.   Urban Realms Model
    c.   Sector Model
    d.   Multiple Nuclei Model
    e.   Concentric Zone Model

FREE-RESPONSE QUESTIONS

Directions: You have 75 minutes to answer all three of the following questions. It is recommended that you spend approximately one-third of your time (25 minutes) on each question. It is suggested that you take up to 5 minutes of this time to plan and outline each answer. While a formal essay is not required, it is not enough to answer a question by merely listing facts. Illustrate your answers with substantive geographic examples where appropriate. Be sure that you number each of your answers, including individual parts, in the answer booklet as the questions are numbered below.

Answer all items using the A, B, C, etc. format

1.   Use the maps to answer the following questions:
   A.   What geographic concept is being shown or demonstrated in the ***set of three maps*** (on this and the next page) of Russellville, Arkansas?
   B.   Using the concept you named in Part A, identify the map that shows the least amount of distance and explain why this is so.
   C.   Explain which map would be most useful in planning a trip from Russellville to Clarksville and which map would be most useful in navigating to Old Post Road Park.

1

2

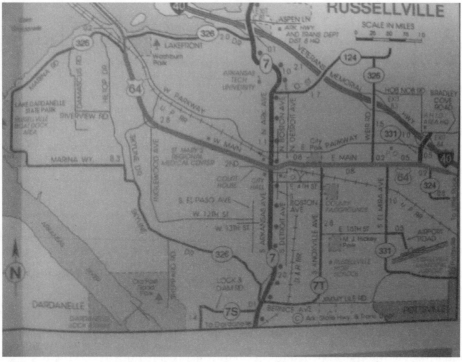

3

Photos of map used by permission of the Arkansas State Highway and Transportation Department, Little Rock, Arkansas. Map published in 2011.

2. Geographers use regions to help define and delimit the similarities and differences in places.
    A. Define formal, functional and perceptual regions.
    B. Give one real-world example of each type of region.
    C. Identify the type of region which is most difficult to define.
    D. Give two real-world examples to explain why this type of region (part C answer) is more difficult to define.

3. Agriculture has been vital for human population growth and expansion.
    A. Explain the geography behind where agriculture originated and explain why it occurred in those locations.
    B. Explain what the Columbian Exchange was.
    C. Take one region of the world and explain how it was impacted by the Columbian Exchange.

AP HUMAN GEOGRAPHY
EXAM TWO

You should allow 60 minutes to choose the BEST answer for each of the following items.

1. The location of a place using the latitude-longitude grid is called:
   a. relative location
   b. absolute location
   c. central location
   d. referenced location
   e. actual location

2. The set of processes that are increasing and deepening interactions, interdependence and relationships is known as _____.
   a. possibilism
   b. spatial interaction
   c. globalization
   d. geocaching
   e. environmental determinism

3. The areas where civilizations developed and innovated are called:
   a. culture systems
   b. primary regions
   c. culture hearths
   d. clustered regions
   e. indigenous area

4.   The diagram below shows an area of interactions and connections that are best described as
     a _____ region.
     a.   perceptual
     b.   formal
     c.   vernacular
     d.   cognitive
     e.   functional

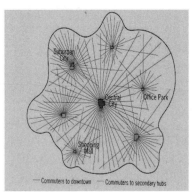

From de Blij and Murphy, *Human Geography, Seventh Edition*, John Wiley and Sons, Inc.

5.   The process of the spreading of an idea from its source area to other cultures is the process of
     cultural:
     a.   possibilism
     b.   simulation
     c.   adaptation
     d.   sharing
     e.   diffusion

6.   The technique where geographers use satellites and aircraft to monitor, among other things,
     environmental changes on the earth's surface is known as:
     a.   remote sensing
     b.   terra incognita
     c.   cultural ecology
     d.   sequent occupance
     e.   perceptual region

7. An outsider traveling into the southern part of the United States might begin to hear slower speech patterns and country/gospel music on the radio, encounter large numbers of Baptist churches, grits on restaurant menus and large front porches on houses. The traveler's thoughts about these characteristics might form the basis of his or her _____ of this place.

    a. perceptual region

    b. formal region

    c. stimulus region

    d. transculturation region

    e. culture hearth

8. Which of the following statements is FALSE concerning the world's population?

    a. Artificial birth control use is higher in core countries.

    b. Population growth rates differ from place to place.

    c. Uneducated women usually have higher fertility rates.

    d. High fertility rates tend to be in overpopulated areas.

    e. Population is evenly distributed over the earth's surface.

9. The *arithmetic* population density for a country is determined by dividing the total:

    a. number of city dwellers by rural people

    b. area of square miles by five

    c. minority population of the area

    d. population by the total land area

    e. population by the number of farmers

10. An age-sex diagram, such as the pyramid below, with a large base, steep sides and a very pointed top most likely indicates a:

    a. slow growth country

    b. gay/lesbian neighborhood

    c. migrant worker community

    d. rapid growth country

    e. city with a prison

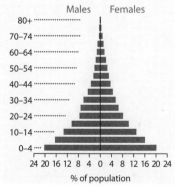

From Fouberg, Murphy, and de Blij, *Human Geography, Tenth Edition*, John Wiley and Sons, Inc.

11. In examining a population density map of East Asia, the pattern of population decline would be from:
    a. south to north
    b. north to south
    c. the interior toward the coast
    d. the coast toward the interior
    e. northern coast to southern coast

12. Migration streams into the U.S.:
    a. were at their lowest point between World War I and World War II.
    b. have increased through every twenty year period since 1840.
    c. came to an apex between 1840-1860 as eastern Europeans arrived.
    d. saw large declines in the 1990s due to Clinton administration policies.
    e. were increased in 1880-1900 as large numbers of Hispanics began to enter.

13. Using your knowledge of population density and distribution, which two of the four boxes below have the highest distribution of triangles?
    a. 1, 2
    b. 3, 4
    c. 4, 1
    d. 2, 3
    e. 2, 4

14. If a population increases by a uniform amount during a series of equal time periods, the increase is said to be:
    a. linear
    b. compounded
    c. exponential
    d. modest
    e. doubling

15. Using your knowledge of natural increase, if a population is growing at an average rate of 2 percent, its doubling time would be approximately _____ years.
    a. 20
    b. 25
    c. 50
    d. 35
    e. 10

16. In 1798, Thomas Malthus published an essay in which he claimed that population increased at a(n) _____ rate, while the means of subsistence grew at a(n) _____ rate.
    a. linear; exponential
    b. cultural; ethnic
    c. arithmetic; geometric
    d. declining; increasing
    e. exponential; linear

17. In which stage of the demographic transition would the age-sex diagram below most likely be located?
    a. 1
    b. 2
    c. 3
    d. 4
    e. 1 or 4

18. The problem with using *arithmetic* population density to investigate the population pattern of a country is that such a density figure does not take into consideration:
    a. annual population increases
    b. internal clustering patterns
    c. annexation of new territory
    d. possible loss of territory
    e. external political forces

19. The long-term relocation of an individual, household, or group to a new location outside the community of origin is called:
    a. resettlement
    b. transportation
    c. migration
    d. transmovement
    e. transhumance

20. An age-sex diagram with high numbers of people in the upper age cohorts is most indicative of a city with:
    a. a large college-aged population
    b. a town devastated by a major tornado
    c. a country with high rates of dowry deaths
    d. a country with very low fertility rates
    e. a city with a large retirement community

21. In the United States during the 1980s and 1990s, internal migration streams were moving generally
    a. from west to east and south to north
    b. from west to east and north to south
    c. completely static
    d. from east to west and south to north
    e. from east to west and north to south

22. A dreadful conflict in which former European country pushed as many as three million people to migrate from their homes in the 1990s?
    a. Poland
    b. Germany
    c. France
    d. Ukraine
    e. Yugoslavia

23. The measure of the number of children born to women of childbearing age in the population is called the:
    a. actual birth rate
    b. crude birth rates
    c. natural increase rate
    d. adjusted birth rate
    e. total fertility rate

24. Which of the following countries would you predict has the highest CDR?
    a. Ukraine
    b. Japan
    c. Indonesia
    d. Sierra Leone
    e. Portugal

25. Ravenstein's Gravity Model of migration stated all of these EXCEPT:
    a. Net migration is only a fraction of gross migration between two places.
    b. The majority of migrants move only a short distance.
    c. Rural residents are far less likely to migrate than their urban counterparts.
    d. Families are less likely to make international moves than young adults.
    e. Migrants who move longer distances tend to choose big city destinations.

26. The most widely used and diffused Indo-European language in the world today is:
    a. English
    b. German
    c. Spanish
    d. French
    e. Basque

27. Which of these best describes the world's religions from largest to smallest?
    a. Christianity – Hinduism – Islam – Sikhism – Judaism
    b. Islam – Christianity – Hinduism – Judaism – Chinese religions
    c. Buddhism – Christianity – Islam – Hinduism – Sikhism
    d. Christianity – Islam – Hinduism – Buddhism – Sikhism
    e. Christianity – Buddhism – Hinduism – Judaism – Islam

28. English is a member of the _____ subfamily of languages.
    a. Romance
    b. Germanic
    c. Slavic
    d. Celtic
    e. Druid

29. The presence of fast food restaurants tends to make a cultural landscape more:
    a. heterogeneous
    b. religious
    c. rural
    d. homogeneous
    e. isolated

30. Wilber Zelinsky attempted to define cultural landscapes/regions by using information found in _____.
    a. signs
    b. ethnicities
    c. cameras
    d. journals
    e. phonebooks

31. The island in the Mediterranean Sea that had to be partitioned because two cultures, the Greeks and Turks, could not get along is:
    a. Malta
    b. Sicily
    c. Corsica
    d. Sardinia
    e. Cyprus

32. The world's most populated Islamic state is:
    a. Iran
    b. Pakistan
    c. Indonesia
    d. the Philippines
    e. Saudi Arabia

33. Which country would most accurately satisfy the definition of a nation-state?
    a. Kurdistan
    b. United States
    c. Japan
    d. Mexico
    e. South Africa

34. The element most essential and common to the world's political states is:
    a. ethnicity
    b. capital
    c. territory
    d. religion
    e. coastline

35. Which of the following phrases BEST defines "stateless nation"?
    a. many ethnic groups within several contiguous states with no one group dominating
    b. a group of people with a common culture and sense of unity but with no territory
    c. a single nation dispersed across and predominant in two or more states
    d. a distinct group of people occupying their own territory and sharing a common set of values
    e. an independent political entity that is not subdivided into regional or local units

36. Many of Europe's unitary states and their administrative frameworks were designed to:
    a. ensure the central government's authority over all parts of the state
    b. allow maximum local autonomy for the citizens of the country
    c. control the core area and let the hinterlands have autonomy
    d. create conditions for a transition to a federal state government
    e. expand the rights of non-majority tribal and linguistic groups

37. Which academic field of inquiry deals with the spatial aspects of voting systems, voting behavior and voter representation?
    a. government geography
    b. electoral geography
    c. congressional geography
    d. apportionment geography
    e. district geography

38. Which of the following is NOT an example of devolution in Europe?
    a. the breakup of Yugoslavia
    b. the "velvet revolution" in Czechoslovakia
    c. local autonomy in Wales from the UK
    d. Basque separatist movement in Spain
    e. the re-unification of East and West Germany

39. The colonial powers delimited the boundaries of _____ at the Conference of Berlin.
    a. Asia
    b. South America
    c. Central America
    d. Africa
    e. Antarctica

40. Geographer K.W. Robinson said that _____ states, "are the most expressive of all types of government" and "do not create unity out of diversity; rather, it enables the two to coexist."
    a. unitary
    b. multicore
    c. primate
    d. federal
    e. tribal

41. MERCOSUR is a supranational organization located in:
    a. Australia
    b. Africa
    c. Europe
    d. Asia
    e. South America

42. Delimited boundaries are best described generally as:
    a. having been officially drawn on a map
    b. being evident by fences, stones, markers, etc.
    c. having been simply described through treaties
    d. are drawn predominantly in geometric lines
    e. following landscape features like rivers

43. The Green Revolution had all of the following EXCEPT:
    a.   increased world cereal grains production
    b.   decreased the overall number of farmers
    c.   decreased the number of jobs available for women
    d.   was instrumental in famine relief
    e.   increased arable land by over 75%

44. _____ agriculture is generally located on the west coasts of continents, and includes the dry, summer climates of southern California, central Chile, South Africa's cape, Greece and other areas, and grow crops such as grapes, citrus, etc.
    a.   Chapparal
    b.   Mediterranean
    c.   Commercial
    d.   Plantation
    e.   Luxury

45. Which of these products had an increase in demand in the 1970s due to more health benefits and the rise of fast food restaurants?
    a.   chicken
    b.   duck
    c.   mutton
    d.   pork
    e.   dairy

46. Plantation agriculture is characterized by all of the following EXCEPT:
    a.   usually grow one crop
    b.   crops are grown largely for export
    c.   farming of subsistence crops by local people
    d.   are located on the best land in the area
    e.   has multinational corporations as owners

47. Poultry production in the United States:
    a.   is spatially oriented to the more rural regions of the country
    b.   decreased with the emergence of conglomerates like Tyson
    c.   occurs naturally in urban areas as von Thünen's model predicts
    d.   dropped because of lower nutritional values in chicken meat
    e.   has been outsourced to countries such as Chile

48. Which of the following agricultural operations is characterized by sizable capital, low labor input per unit of land, large land units, and medium/long distance from market?
    a. intensive subsistence farming
    b. shifting cultivation
    c. commercial wheat farming
    d. patch agriculture
    e. hunting/gathering

49. Which Asian country owes its vast cotton fields/production to the influence of colonial Britain?
    a. Pakistan
    b. Sri Lanka
    c. the Philippines
    d. India
    e. Bangladesh

50. Which of the following is NOT an example of shifting agriculture?
    a. metes and bounds
    b. slash and burn
    c. swidden
    d. milpa
    e. patch

51. According to von Thünen's *original* model, which of the following would you expect to find farthest from the market?
    a. strawberries
    b. cattle
    c. tomatoes
    d. corn
    e. forest belt

52. Which of the following is FALSE about organic agriculture?
    a. The markets for these products are largely located in core countries.
    b. Market prices are low since the costs of organic agriculture remain low.
    c. Organic agriculture reduces the amount of chemicals put into the soil and water.
    d. Some countries are approaching 10 percent sales figures of organic agriculture.
    e. Taste and health benefits are two reasons why many demand organic products.

53. The system of measuring land which usually had a starting point from rivers, canals and roads was the:
    a. long lot
    b. feudal
    c. township-and-range
    d. village
    e. metes-and-bounds

54. Each of the following statements about suburbanization is correct EXCEPT:
    a. the high number of World War II soldier casualties limited the demand for housing for a decade
    b. the completion of the interstate highway system made commuting to the workplace easier
    c. industry was attracted to the suburbs by modern plant facilities and plenty of parking spaces for employees
    d. service industries developed as a result of the purchasing power and the available suburban labor force
    e. as people moved to the suburbs, regional shopping centers replaced the CBD retail districts

55. The population growth center in the United States from 1790 to the present has generally:
    a. moved north and south
    b. moved west and east
    c. moved north and east
    d. moved east and west
    e. moved south and west

56. The poor living conditions of European manufacturing cities were eventually improved by government intervention, legislation, recognition of workers' rights and the introduction of:
    a. city planning and zoning
    b. more efficient factories
    c. a substitute for coal
    d. suburbanization
    e. blockbusting

57. According to the text, the earliest civilization occurred in:
    a. Andean America
    b. Indus Valley
    c. Mediterranean Europe
    d. Mesopotamia
    e. Nile Valley

58. A town is defined as a place where an assemblage of goods/services is available with a:
    a. good highway system
    b. minimum of 25,000 people
    c. public transportation system
    d. hinterland
    e. recognizable suburban area

59. According to the text, the dominant city of the North American interior is:
    a. Kansas City
    b. St. Louis
    c. Cleveland
    d. Denver
    e. Chicago

60. The spatial process of clustering by commercial enterprises for mutual advantage and benefit is called:
    a. relocation
    b. diffusion
    c. gravitation
    d. agglomeration
    e. blockbusting

61. Harris and Ullman's multiple nuclei model of urban structure arose from the idea that _____ was losing its dominant position in the metropolitan city to other competition.
    a. the exurb
    b. the edge city
    c. public transportation
    d. the suburb
    e. the CBD

62. The Latin American City Structure Model below has all of the following elements EXCEPT:
    a. squatter areas located on the outer ring of the city
    b. very poor people living close to the very wealthy
    c. a mall area characterized by open pedestrian zones
    d. distinct upper income suburbs located on the periphery
    e. gangs and drug lords located in the Perifico

A NEW AND IMPROVED MODEL OF LATIN AMERICAN CITY STRUCTURE

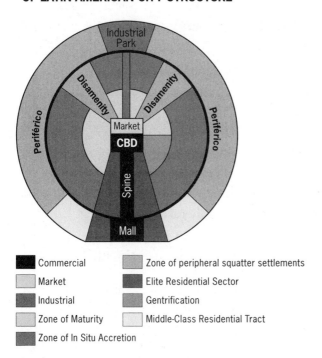

- Commercial
- Market
- Industrial
- Zone of Maturity
- Zone of In Situ Accretion
- Zone of peripheral squatter settlements
- Elite Residential Sector
- Gentrification
- Middle-Class Residential Tract

From Fouberg, Murphy, and de Blij, *Human Geography, Tenth Edition*, John Wiley and Sons, Inc. Adapted with permission from: L. Ford, "A New and Improved Model of Latin American City Structure," *The Geographical Review* 86 (1996), p. 438.

63. The sector model of urban structure by Homer Hoyt promoted what important aspects of urban structure and life?
    a. neighborhood ethnicity/socioeconomics
    b. bid rent/transport routes
    c. gender studies/gay-lesbian neighborhoods
    d. public housing/poor people
    e. irrelevance of the CBD/edge cities

64. The _____ model illustrates the theoretical idea that two vendors selling ice cream on a beach would eventually be selling back-to-back to maximize the number of customers and profits.
    a. Burgess
    b. Weber
    c. Hotelling
    d. Losch
    e. Hoyt

65. Which of the following is NOT a characteristic of a "periphery country" in the capitalist economic system?
    a. narrower range of consumer products than in core countries
    b. exporting of high quality finished goods
    c. less advanced technology
    d. lower wages than core countries
    e. exporting of raw materials to core countries

66. Which of the terms listed below describes the entrenchment of the old system of dominance by core countries on periphery countries under an economic rather than direct political/military control?
    a. colonialism
    b. developing dominance
    c. neo-colonialism
    d. transhumance
    e. neo-nihilism

67. _____ Theory declares that prosperity is sustained in the core, while poverty is sustained in the periphery.
    a. Organic
    b. Modernization
    c. Dependency
    d. Secondary
    e. Time-Space Convergence

68. The principal structuralist alternative to Rostow's model of economic development is known as:
    a. the "takeoff" model
    b. the liberal model
    c. the modernization model
    d. dependency theory
    e. least cost theory

69. Extractive activities are a synonym for _____ activities.
    a. primary
    b. secondary
    c. tertiary
    d. quaternary
    e. quinary

70. The economic boom on East Asia's Pacific Rim is based substantially on low-cost
    _____.
    a. raw materials
    b. transportation
    c. labor
    d. power
    e. food

71. Outsourcing call center services to India is done for all of the following reasons EXCEPT:
    a. stable democracy
    b. English speakers
    c. transport costs
    d. college graduates
    e. labor costs

72. For most goods, the cheapest method of transport over short distances is by:
    a. railroad
    b. truck
    c. ship
    d. pipeline
    e. air

73. In northern Mexico's border region with the United States, there is a manufacturing zone where plants, mainly owned by U.S. companies, transform imported, duty-free components or raw materials into finished industrial products. These plants are called:
    a. maquiladoras
    b. braceros
    c. pulques
    d. favelas
    e. bulk-reducers

74. According to the text, which of the following city sets contains the three most dominant World Cities?
    a.   London-Tokyo-Beijing
    b.   New York-London-Tokyo
    c.   Shanghai-Paris-New York
    d.   Tokyo-London-Paris
    e.   Los Angeles-New York-Chicago

75. A location along transport routes where goods must be transferred from one mode to another is known as a(n)?
    a.   maquiladora
    b.   agglomeration
    c.   technopole
    d.   break-of-bulk
    e.   buffer zone

FREE-RESPONSE QUESTIONS

Directions: You have 75 minutes to answer all three of the following questions. It is recommended that you spend approximately one-third of your time (25 minutes) on each question. It is suggested that you take up to 5 minutes of this time to plan and outline each answer. While a formal essay is not required, it is not enough to answer a question by merely listing facts. Illustrate your answers with substantive geographic examples where appropriate. Be sure that you number each of your answers, including individual parts, in the answer booklet as the questions are numbered below.

Answer all items using the A, B, C, etc. format

1. Von Thünen's model is an important concept in the geography of agriculture. Answer the following prompts about this model:
    A. Define market gardening.
    B. Where does market gardening fit into von Thünen's model?
    C. Give 3 examples of market garden products.
    D. For each of the items named in C, give the reason why that product would be produced at that location.

2. Languages and language issues are a major topic of study in cultural geography. Answer the following items about languages.
    A. Define lingua franca, pidgin and Creole.
    B. Using the tables and your knowledge of population, diffusion, language or other factors, choose two (2) languages which have changed and give 2 full explanations for each from Tables 1, 2 and/or 3 and **fully explain** possible reasons for the differences over time.

World Language Rankings – Global Number of Speakers

Table 1

1994-95

1. Mandarin Chinese	4. Hindi
2. English	5. Russian
3. Spanish	6. Bengali

Source: Human Geography – de Blij & Murphy, 6th edition

Table 2

2002-2003

1. Mandarin Chinese	4. Spanish
2. English	5. Arabic
3. Hindi	6. Bengali

Source: Human Geography – de Blij & Murphy, 7th edition

Table 3

2011

1. Mandarin	6. Bengali (tie)
2. Spanish	7. Portuguese (tie)
3. English	8. Russian
4. Arabic	9. Japanese
5. Hindi	10. German

Source: http://geography.about.com/od/culturalgeography/a/10languages.htm

3.   Today's world is a balance between the global and the local.

A.   Describe one specific technology from the 20th/21st century and explain how it has helped make the world a more connected place.

B.   Describe one specific technology from the 20th/21st century and explain how it has helped maintain local cultures.